GREAT WAR BRITAIN

SHEFFIELD

Remembering 1914–18

SHEFFIELD

Remembering 1914–18

TIM LYNCH

Frontispiece:

Sheffield City War Memorial
(Beth Lynch)

First published 2015

The History Press
The Mill, Brimscombe Port
Stroud, Gloucestershire, GL5 2QG
www.thehistorypress.co.uk

British Library Cataloguing in Publication Data.
A catalogue record for this book is available from the British Library.

ISBN 978 0 7509 6048 9

Typesetting and origination by The History Press
Printed in Malta by Melita Press

CONTENTS

Timeline

1914

28 June

Assassination of Archduke Franz Ferdinand in Sarajevo

4 August

Great Britain declares war on Germany

23 August

Battle of Tannenberg commences

6 September

First Battle of the Marne

10 September

Sheffield University and City Special Battalion recognised by the War Office

19 October

First Battle of Ypres

1915

25 January

The Lord Mayor of Sheffield issues instructions for citizens in case of 'visits by hostile aircraft'

22 April

Lord Kitchener acknowledges 'Sheffield is doing things of immense value to the state'

25 April

Allied landing at Gallipoli

7 May

Germans torpedo and sink the Lusitania

31 May

First German Zeppelin raid on London

20 December

Allies finish their evacuation of and withdrawal from Gallipoli

1916

24 January

The British Government introduces conscription

1 February

Germany falsely claims to have bombed Sheffield

21 February

Battle of Verdun commences

31 May

Battle of Jutland

4 June

Brusilov Offensive commence

1 July

First day of the Battle of the Somme with 57,000 British casualties

Sheffield City Batallion suffers 468 men killed, wounded or missing on the first day of the Somme offensive

27 August

Italy declares war on Germany

25 September

Twenty-nine people are killed in a Zeppelin attack on 'a north Midland town'

18 December

Battle of Verdun ends

1917

6 April

The United States declares war on Germany

9 April

Battle of Arras

31 July

Third Battle of Ypres (Passchendaele)

20 August

Third Battle of Verdun

24 September

Thomas Leenane is sent to prison for a month for giving a German prisoner of war a tin of milk

26 October

Second Battle of Passchendaele

20 November

Battle of Cambrai

7 December

USA declares war on Austria-Hungary

1918

28 February

Sheffield City Battalion is disbanded

3 March

*Russia and the Central Powers
sign the Treaty of Brest-Litovsk*

21 March

Second Battle of the Somme

4 July

*US troops give a baseball demonstration
at Bramall Lane football ground*

15 July

Second Battle of the Marne

8 August

*Battle of Amiens, first stage of
the Hundred Days Offensive*

22 September

The Great Allied Balkan victory

27 September

Storming of the Hindenburg Line

8 November

Armistice negotiations commence

9 November

*Kaiser Wilhelm II abdicates,
Germany is declared a republic*

11 November

*Sheffield records 402 deaths from
influenza in the past week*

*Armistice Day, cessation of hostilities
on the Western Front*

1919

28 January

*Approximately 1,400 Belgian
refugees leave Sheffield to return home*

17 July

*Sheffield children celebrate
peace with a grand pageant*

ACKNOWLEDGEMENTS

Research for a book of this kind relies heavily on the kindness of a great many people. I have been fortunate to have the assistance of the staff of Sheffield Libraries and Archives, the Sheffield 1914–18 Project and the opportunity to swap stories with Kate Linderholm of BBC Radio Sheffield, whose work on the stories of South Yorkshire during the Great War has produced a fascinating insight into local life in those turbulent years.

Fran Cantillion at The History Press offered me the chance to write this book and has been supportive throughout a some-times turbulent process. Fellow Yorkshire authors in the series Lucy Moore and Kathryn Hughes have been generous in passing on any snippets of their work that related to Sheffield and have produced their own works in this series.

Most of all my thanks, as ever, go to my patient family. To Jacqueline, for keeping things together when I was off in my own little world. To Josh, for realising that frequent demands for drinks, toast and conversations about Spiderman are essential to any creative project. My thanks in particular to Beth Lynch for research work and her photography.

Uncredited photographs are taken from the author's collection. It has not been possible to identify copyright holders for the images used and no infringement is intended

INTRODUCTION

In late 1917, the Revd William Odom wrote:

In the autumn of 1915, every person in the country was required to register so that they could be assessed by the Ministry of Labour. Those in certain vital industries were marked with a star to indicate they should not be called up for the forces.

NATIONAL REGISTRATION ACT, 1915.

For nearly three years, there has raged the most terrible war the world has ever witnessed – one in which its five continents are involved. Everywhere mighty upheavals and changes, dramatic and unexpected, are taking place in national, social, commercial, and religious life. In addition to the great world Empires, other lands, the names of which are familiar to Bible readers, as Egypt, Sinai, Palestine, Salonika (Thessalonica), and Mesopotamia (cradle of the human race), are entangled in the terrible conflict.

Apart from the unspeakable tragedies by land and sea, confiscation, deportation, and slavery, innumerable deaths on the battlefield and in hospitals, huge liners, hospital ships, and merchant vessels have been torpedoed and mined, towns and villages laid in ruinous heaps, cathedrals and churches ruthlessly wrecked, countless homes ruined, and fruitful fields transformed into desert wastes ... In this gigantic struggle the killed and wounded are numbered by millions. At the close of 1916 in the burial grounds of France and Belgium the bodies of more than 150,000 brave British soldiers lay at rest.

The cost in money to our own nation alone has increased to seven million daily, besides which vast sums are being voluntarily contributed to war charities … From July, 1914, the history of the British Empire is crowded with records of heroic actions and unparalleled sacrifices in the sacred cause of liberty, truth, and righteousness. For love of country brave men and youths have freely offered all they could – their lives … To-day, myriads of wives and parents hold their husbands and lads who have fallen 'in proud and loving memory'.

In this terrible struggle Sheffield has taken a foremost place. Not to speak of the thousands who have offered themselves for active service, there has been the great army of workers at home – men, women, and girls in our large works forging weapons of war, thus transforming our city into the greatest arsenal in the world…The war has not only discovered new and unexpected powers, and made men – brave men – but it has also revealed heroes. We are learning that it is not what a man gains that makes him great, it is what he gives.

In 1914, Britain went to war. A century on, historians still argue the rights and wrongs of that decision. Whether for better or worse, the war undoubtedly changed the world. Every man, woman and child in Britain was affected and their sacrifices, great and small, would mean that life in Britain would never be the same again. On every battlefield on land, sea and in the air, the people of Sheffield would come to know only too well the true cost of that change. They would also come to know a new front line as the killing spread beyond the battlefield and into their very homes.

From the Sheaf to the Somme, this is the story of Sheffield at war.

Tim Lynch, 2015

1

'DAMNED BAD PLACE, SHEFFIELD'

– King George III

At the start of the twentieth century, even the most loyal citizens agreed that Sheffield, for all its great wealth and its vital importance to the steel and iron industry that had built the British Empire, was not a beautiful city: writing on a history of the city on behalf of the Sheffield Education Committee in 1915, Alderman John Derry, one-time editor of the Sheffield Independent wrote:

> People who have only passed by the city in the trains that run through its central valley … think of it as a crowded, ugly place, drearily blackened by smoke during the day, and lighted by the wavering glare of many furnace fires; and they sometimes say to each other: 'How can people pass their lives in a town like this?'

POPULATION
In 1911, Sheffield's population was young. Of the 454,632 people in 99,069 households recorded by the census that year, 53,884 were aged under 4 and 148,351 – almost a third – were under 15.

Sheffield may be, as Derry claimed, 'one of the most beautifully situated inland cities in the world', but even he admitted that 'its appearance at a glance is not attractive'. It was a comment that Charles Compton Reade, a New Zealand-born journalist and town planner, wholeheartedly agreed with:

In contrast to the wooded hills and the long radiant valleys, nothing could be more powerful or dramatic than the historic and busy centre of Sheffield. Placed as it is in a neighbourhood of wondrous charm and sylvan glory, the city and its immediate environment are hopelessly unbeautiful. From the eminence of Victoria Station, the eye is greeted by a sea of blackened roofs and chimney pots straggling from a gloomy valley to the hills beyond. It lies before one naked in ugliness, what with its miles of crooked and cranky streets, its endless chimney shafts and slated roofs crowding in from remote horizon to the eminence, where the Town Hall points a ponderous and sooty tower to the smoke-stained skies ...

Writing at about the same time, historian J.S. Fletcher described Yorkshire as a county 'of almost violent contrasts' and nowhere was this truer than in Sheffield itself. Those who could afford to lived on the western edges of town, where the prevailing wind blew across the moors and swept the smoke and pollution eastwards over the crowded slums of the city centre, home to the vast majority of workers. According to records, 27.53 metric tons of air pollution were recorded in each square kilometre of Attercliffe in June 1914 alone. Across the city, an average of 12.86 metric tons per square kilometre per month made Sheffield one of the most polluted cities in the country and it was claimed that the smoke-filled air blocked out a quarter of all sunlight. Between 1801 and 1913 the population had grown from 45,755 to 471,662 as people flocked to Sheffield in search of work, but the new arrivals found a city struggling to accommodate them, adding to the misery of life in the slums.

Compton Reade wrote in 1911:

The houses and streets for the most part in these areas are revoltingly dirty. Nothing could be more repulsive or indicative of the evils that have arisen with the growth of the factory system in England, than some of these historic thoroughfares of Sheffield ... Overhead the smoke hangs in a listless brown canopy in the sunlight. In the hot, humid streets and the long, black buildings the fierce, relentless activities of men and women pass unceasingly, and the making of great riches on the one hand and greater poverty on the other tells its story afresh. One looks for beauty in vain. It fled to the hills years ago – the hills where there are so many fine homes and bright, clean faces. Is it not enough to make us wonder how far the riches of the one are the price of the other?

It was said that smoke blocked out up to 25 per cent of sunlight and tons of pollution from thousands of chimneys covered the city every day.

That was a question being asked by many in the city's crowded slums, where diseases were common and spread rapidly. By 1900, one in five children died before their first birthday, most often from diarrhoea caused by polluted drinking water or spread in summer by flies swarming from the overflowing privies shared by whole rows of cramped terrace houses. Those children that survived showed an alarming range of physical health problems associated with poor diet and a lack of fresh air that would create problems for military recruiters in the years to come. Already, the Boer War had highlighted the number of potential recruits from urban areas falling short of the basic medical standard required for service in the army. Alarmed by the 'moral and physical deterioration' of the British population, efforts began to improve health and hygiene by providing parks and sports facilities, free education and school meals as well as an old age pension. With few homes having plumbing, public baths provided the only opportunity for citizens to wash, rarely more often than once per week. As newspapers debated the experimental idea of mixed bathing at Rotherham swimming pools, Sheffield offered a two price deal: bathers paid tuppence on clean water days, a penny the rest of the week.

It was very much a divided city. Of the 454,632 people recorded in the 1911 census, only 69,807 were eligible to vote, but Sheffield was rapidly becoming a centre for political action. In 1908 more days were lost to industrial action than in the entire previous decade and in 1909, a series of strikes hit the coal industry, causing Home Secretary Winston Churchill to order troops into South Wales to restore peace among the 30,000 striking miners after Prime Minister H.H. Asquith made it clear that the government would use all its resources to enforce order. So began 'the great unrest', as between 1910 and 1914 the number of industrial disputes across the country rocketed, reaching a peak of 872 in 1912 with 40 million days lost to strikes – ten times the total of any previous year. Determined to crack down on strikers, the government sent in troops to keep order but the move only heightened tensions and in Liverpool and Llanelli soldiers fired into attacking mobs, killing demonstrators. Like every other industrial town, Sheffield saw armed soldiers on the streets as men of the Gordon Highlanders were called out from Hillsborough Barracks to restore order and keep the peace, causing trades union leaders to call on local men not to join the part-time Territorial Force because it was felt they would be called upon to shoot striking workers.

The main concern for most people, though, was the gangs roaming Sheffield's streets. The letters pages of the *Sheffield Telegraph* in August 1913 were filled with complaints about the Gas Tank Gang, the Mooneys, the Park Gang and others who had brought what was described as 'a state of terrorism that one would have imagined impossible in a city the size of Sheffield in the twentieth century'. One correspondent, signing off as

'Coal getters', many of them children straight from school, fought hard for a living wage of 8s a day. When war broke out, few could afford the drop to a soldier's basic wage of just 1s a day.

'Englishman', wrote of being prepared to fight back and stand up to the bullies. Soon after, another letter advised 'any person who has business that keeps him about town, especially at night, to spend a shilling or two in a revolver and a few cartridges and if attacked by any of these gangs to laugh at the nonsense of "Englishman" about using their fists and SHOOT'. Fights that involved smashed glasses as weapons were common and shocked magistrates responsible for the granting of licences heard that even in 'respectable' pubs, landlords routinely armed themselves with pistols for protection against armed gangs. Gun and knife crime remained a common feature of news stories in the coming years. In February 1916, for example, 20 year olds Harold Hensop and Clifford Hirst were both fined for firing shots into the air 'as a joke'. Both told the court that they routinely carried pistols 'for protection'. 'As we look back over 1913,' wrote the Revd P.D. Woods in the *Royston Parish Magazine* at the end of the year, 'we must all feel that it was a year marked by a spirit of unrest … Most of us, I feel sure, will not regret the dawning of 1914.'

> Sheffield University allowed women to attend and to earn full degrees from 1905. By 1918 it had women lecturers. Meanwhile, Cambridge University only awarded its first degrees to women in 1948.

Unfortunately for the Revd Woods and his parishioners, 1914 brought no respite. In February, bombs 'of an Irish Republican type' were planted at the Leeds Municipal Power Station and at Harewood Territorial Barracks, where police reinforcements were being housed during yet another large-scale strike – this time of Corporation workers – and the chief suspect was an Irishman seen nearby shouting anti-British slogans. Soon after, poorly worded orders were issued to troops in Ireland to prevent military arms stores being seized in case of the expected nationalist uprising. These were interpreted as orders to fight Unionist volunteers, whose stated aim was the protection of British interests in Ireland and which were seen by many officers as linked closely to the army's own purpose there. As a result, the government faced a possible large-scale mutiny by the Curragh garrison that was only averted by the diplomatic leadership of a number of senior officers. As the government struggled to deal with the threat of civil war in Ireland and fears that it might spill over to the large Irish population living in England's industrial towns, around 400,000 railwaymen were threatening national strike action at the same time as 200,000 Yorkshire miners were striking to demand a minimum of 7*s* 11*d* a day for 'coal getters'.

Militant suffragettes had launched a series of actions targeting political leaders. There were widespread arson and bomb attacks on private properties around the country and, in May 1914, a bomb was planted at the pump house of the Upper Windledon reservoir near Penistone which, had it exploded, would potentially have put the village of Dunford Bridge at serious risk. So widespread was the campaign of vandalism that one man, charged with smashing a shop window, was condemned for his behaviour and asked by the judge if he thought he was a suffragette. Against a backdrop of industrial unrest, political violence and the growing threat of civil war in Ireland as arguments over the Home Rule Bill came to a head, the assassination of an obscure Austrian Archduke in faraway Sarajevo seemed to be of little importance to the people of Sheffield …

SHEFFIELD: ARMOURER TO THE WORLD
Henry VIII was the first to encourage the manufacturers of South Yorkshire to develop the skills of cannon making. By the turn of the nineteenth century, local mills were turning out guns and cannonballs for Wellington's army and Nelson's navy. By 1914, Sheffield was home to the largest munitions industry in the world.

At 10.45 a.m. on 28 June 1914, Austrian Archduke Franz Ferdinand and his wife Sophie left the Town Hall in Sarajevo in a motorcade heading for the city's hospital. Earlier that morning two Serbian nationalists posted on the route into the city had decided at the last moment not to act but a third nearby had thrown a bomb at Ferdinand's car, which skidded across the car's roof and under the car behind, wounding at least sixteen bystanders. After reading a speech – the paper spattered with blood – at the Town Hall as planned, Ferdinand asked to change the itinerary and to go to visit the wounded in hospital. The driver took the car down a wrong turning and directly into the path of 19-year-old Gavrilo Princip, another member of the Serbian group intending to kill him that day. Princip fired two shots, hitting both Franz Ferdinand and Sophie. Both victims remained seated upright, but died while being driven to the governor's residence for medical treatment. As reported by Count Harrach, Franz Ferdinand's last words were 'Sophie, Sophie! Don't die! Live for our children!' Sophie was dead on arrival at the governor's residence. Franz Ferdinand died ten minutes later.

The murders shocked the world and set in motion a chain of events that would lead to war within weeks, but for the time being, Sheffielders were more concerned when the heatwave that had baked Sheffield for the last month broke at 6 p.m. on the evening of 1 July with a severe storm that brought torrential rain for over an hour and three hours of lightning. 'The Wicker,' reported the *Telegraph*, 'was like a great river for half an hour', and cellars in Attercliffe, Neepsend, Heeley and Sheaf Street flooded as the main sewer, unable to cope with the volume of water, burst outside the Upperthorpe Library. A young woman in Field's Cafe, terrified by 'a vivid flash followed by a heavy crash of thunder', collapsed and was taken to hospital, whilst another fainted on the platform of the Midland Station. Two houses on Wynyard Road were struck by lightning and Mr Timperley of Hills Farm at Dronfield had a narrow escape as lightning blasted through concrete flooring in the farmyard.

Clearing up after the storm occupied locals for the next week or two, by which time events in Europe were spiralling out of control. Austria, supported by Germany, blamed Serbia for the killings. Serbia, backed by Russia, denied involvement. Throughout July, the dispute escalated until Germany and Russia mobilised their armies. At the end of the month Russia offered to negotiate a demobilisation but it was too late. On 1 August, Germany declared war. France, tied to Russia by a mutual protection alliance, was forced to mobilise its forces before Germany could execute its long-standing plan to invade France via neutral Belgium. On 2 August Germany invaded Luxemburg and on the following day declared war on France. On 4 August, claiming to be responding to a French attack, the Germans invaded Belgium. Having been one of the guarantors of Belgian neutrality, Britain was now forced to act. With a massive overseas empire, Britain could not allow international law to be flouted, nor could it allow Germany, the only naval power in the world able to challenge the Royal Navy, to establish itself in the English Channel where, once France was defeated, there would be no barrier to an invasion of England.

Over the Bank Holiday weekend, orders were published in the local papers to recall army and navy reservists as Britain, too, began to mobilise. Although the impression today is of a nation excited by the thought of war, there was a great deal of open opposition, with *The Worker* of 1 August declaring that: 'The war is no concern of the working class and their duty is to take every advantage of such lapses into insanity by the capitalist class.' Writing for many, Thomas Cox Meech wrote to the *Sheffield Independent* on 3 August to ask 'Can we keep out of it with honour?' On the same day, 'AHW' also wrote to the paper: 'War is murder. It is the reign of hell on Earth. Workers, will you allow it? … It is our immediate duty to make practical protest against this act of criminal folly – the European war.' But by then it was too late. At midnight on 4 August, after Germany ignored British demands to withdraw from Belgium, war was declared.

Immediately, food prices rocketed as panic buying hit shops everywhere after people stocked up in expectation of a possible German invasion. Flour, sugar and butter costs rose to such a degree that within days the government was forced to step in to control prices. By the following Saturday, Lipton Ltd took out an advert in the *Sheffield Telegraph*: 'We hope the Public will only buy their ordinary weekly supply and assist us as much as possible to keep down Prices.' Banks closed to protect gold reserves and only reopened on the following Friday to allow wages to be paid, although in a new sort of money: instead of coins, new £1 and 10*s* notes had been introduced that needed some explanation:

The issue by the government of the £1 and 10s notes will be a big relief to the gold. The notes were issued in London yesterday and some were received by the Yorkshire Penny Bank from their head offices in London … The alteration from coins to paper money will make no difference. The notes will be offered and accepted in payment just the same as gold and should be treated by the public with the same confidence. Wages paid in paper will have exactly the same purchasing power as if paid in gold and workers need have no hesitation in accepting them … The new £1 notes are printed on small slips of paper 2½in by 5in. They bear the following wording printed in Old English type:

These notes are a legal tender for a payment of any amount. Issued by the Lords Commissioners of His Majesty's Treasury under authority of Act of Parliament
ONE POUND
(Sd) John Bradbury
Secretary to the Treasury
On the left hand side they bear the King's portrait amid ornamentation encircled by the inscription 'Georgius V DG Britt Om Rex FD Ind Imp'. The notes are printed on white paper, watermarked with the royal cipher.

Sheffield in a Trench

In 1917, an anonymous poem, signed only 'A Sheffield Lad', appeared in the press not only in Britain, but across all English-speaking countries. Even after three years of war, it explains why Sheffield men had volunteered for service:

Misr would I like to see? No fear!
Not London – no, nor Windermere,
Nor Paris with its sky so clear –
Give me a look at Sheffield.

I have it in my mental eye –
Its valleys, and its uplands high,
Its smoke-cloud flung against the sky –
The smoke that blackens Sheffield.

Its five small rills that slowly steal
Past rolling-mill and grinding-wheel –
Their very names can make me feel
That I belong to Sheffield.

O Loxley, Rivelin, Porter, Sheaf!
Flow onward to the Don, your chief !
And ripple out your challenge brief –
Men must be free in Sheffield !

I know each tower and lofty dome
That's long made Sheffield air its home.
And where some others, lately come,
Have reared their heads in Sheffield.

I mark each street and winding lane –
Oh, yes, they're black! Oh, yes, they're plain!
But let me tread them once again,
And Heaven will shine in Sheffield.

And I can hear, as luck may hap,
The nickerpecker's* 'tap, tap, tap',
The grindstone's hiss, the tilt's 'rap, rap',
As if I was in Sheffield.

Aye, and the blunt old Sheffield speech
As none else to my soul can reach –
It knows not how to beg, beseech,
The tongue that's spoke in Sheffield.

Could I but see that smoke-cap thick,
Meet swarfy-breech'd Tom and Dick,
And lads with scissors on a stick,
I'd know I was in Sheffield.

But here we are ! – 'What for?' You say
To teach the Boche the time of day,
And keep him far enough away
From setting foot in Sheffield.

A SHEFFIELD LAD
1917

* Sheffield filecutter

Sheffield men still in the army or Royal Naval Reserve left immediately and within days some were in France with the British Expeditionary Force. More followed over the coming weeks as the forces prepared for the massive expansion that would be needed to stand up to the huge German and Austrian armies. Also being marched away were 108 local men of German origin rounded up under the Aliens Act and sent to what the government referred to as 'concentration camps' although some, like Lofthouse Park in Wakefield, were so comfortable that wealthier prisoners paid extra to be held there. Sheffield women who had married German-born men found that they were legally regarded as having taken his nationality and were now 'enemy aliens' in their own country. With their husbands now imprisoned, they were left to manage as best they could, either running the family business or relying on charitable handouts. Some were forced into the workhouse. At the same time, other local men were also being rounded up as enemy aliens – this time by the Germans. Among them were around twenty-five Sheffield men and others from around the city, including Wilhelm Schohnut, a Rotherham-born member of the pork butcher dynasty whose

A cheerful group of enemy aliens being marched into what they hoped would be temporary captivity, August 1914. They would not see their homes again for four years.

shops were spread throughout South Yorkshire. Ironically, whilst members of the family came under attack by neighbours in Britain for being German, Wilhelm was imprisoned by the Germans for being British.

Meanwhile, lurid reports filled British newspapers with tales of the 'rape of Belgium' as the German Army advanced. Most were wildly exaggerated or completely fictional, but there was a strong element of truth behind them. In late August, German troops had killed thirty-eight civilians in the bombardment of the town of Lise, even though by then the town had been in German hands for two weeks. Another 631 men and boys were taken to Germany as forced labour and the rest of the town's 4,000 citizens were forced across the border into neutral Holland. At Malines, around 150 were executed in response to an alleged sniper attack and at Andenne 200 civilians were shot and the town set ablaze. At Dinant, in reprisal for claims that Belgian civilians had tried to hamper German troops repairing a bridge, 612 men, women and children were herded into the town square and shot, the youngest identified victim being just three weeks old. The litany went on, culminating in orders to raze the city of Louvain, where 230,000 priceless books were destroyed when the university's medieval library was set ablaze.

Thousands of Belgian civilians fled the onslaught by travelling to Britain and by late 1914, Folkestone had taken in 26,000 refugees in a single week. On 17 September, an appeal was launched in Sheffield to provide food, clothing and money to help as forty-seven civilian refugees arrived to a sympathetic welcome and a new home at Shirle Hill in Sharrow. Over the coming months, hundreds more would follow: Firvale House was given over to house 150 people and the Norfolk base of the Midland Railway another 180, whilst more were placed in empty properties or lodged with families around the city. A special office was opened at No. 84 The Wicker where, between 11 a.m. and 12.30 p.m.

ALIENS IN BRITAIN.

OFFICIAL ADVICE TO GERMANS AND OTHERS.

"Advice to Aliens now in Britain" was yesterday issued by the British Government as below :—

German subjects must all register themselves at the nearest police station. British women who have married Germans have become German citizens, and must be registered. The children of such marriages are in a similar position.

Foreigners desirous to leave will find no difficulty, unless German subjects, if they provide themselves with passports, etc., and make sure beforehand of boat and train services.

No German subject may leave these shores without special permit from the Secretary of State. Males of military age will not be granted such permits. Others must apply in person or through persons representing them (solicitors or others), or in the case of those living at a distance from London by letter to the Secretary, Home Office, Whitehall, London, S.W. Such applications should be supported by documentary evidence as to identification, employment, etc.

Permits are granted only to leave Britain by certain ports and on a given date by a given steamship service. Therefore those applying should make sure of being able to leave a day or two before.

'Advice to Aliens' was published in every local newspaper. This notification dates from August 1914.

each day, hosts could bring their refugees to sort out problems and have their clothes repaired or replaced. 'The University staff and students,' reported the *Sheffield Yearbook*, 'have provided two houses in Western Bank for a certain number of Belgian families of culture and refinement'.

Aware that many of the refugees were from mining areas, unions in Yorkshire and South Wales made it clear that they would be unwelcome and the refugees themselves were warned not to take British jobs or to work for less than the standard wage. As foreigners, finding work in Sheffield's munitions factories could also prove difficult due to the restrictions put in place by the government although eventually some 'friendly aliens' found work there. Inevitably, complaints about able-bodied Belgians who were out of work began to circulate. Locals were warned that many were 'peasants' and needed to be looked after: 'Sir,' a letter from a reader to the *Telegraph* read, 'Would you kindly draw the attention of your readers to the evil of giving Belgians drinks? They are not accustomed to our beer and we have heard of more than one instance when it has proved too much for them.' When cases came to light

A souvenir postcard commemorating the arrival of Belgian refugees in Sheffield.

An artist's impression of the shelling of Scarborough. The attack on the seaside resort shocked the nation and brought the war home to the people of Yorkshire.

of a few Belgians drinking and getting into trouble, the whole group became tarred with the same brush. 'And how are your Belgian atrocities?' became a common question among those who had offered shelter in the heady days of 1914, only to find the novelty wearing off very quickly.

That November, the fear of Zeppelin attacks meant that bonfires and fireworks were forbidden under the new Defence of the Realm Act and, as Christmas approached, a new threat loomed when a German naval raid took place on the east coast, bombarding Whitby, Scarborough and Hartlepool. The raid killed 137 people and wounded 592, among them 43-year-old Sheffield-born Miss McEntyre, killed when a shell hit her bedroom as she comforted the baby son of friends. It was proof, according to the *Telegraph*, that 'the war has come home to the people of Yorkshire with a vengeance'.

It was clear to even the most optimistic that the war would not be over by Christmas, but Sheffielders were determined not to ignore the season. The annual Christmas fair next to the Midland railway station was well attended and one seller alone hoped to sell 12,000 Christmas trees as people showed their determination to carry on as normal. After months of bad news, there were the occasional brighter moments. On Christmas Eve, the Rabjohn family of Meersbrook Bank Road received a postcard. Missing since 22 September, Corporal Arthur Rabjohn had written to his wife and two children from a German prison camp with news that he was safe and well: 'Don't spoil your Christmas on my account,' he wrote, 'enjoy yourselves as I am alright.'

As 1914 drew to a close, Sheffield was preparing to play its part in the Great European War. A lot would be asked of it …

2

'THE POST OF HONOUR WAS AT CATCLIFFE ...'

In 1906, the writer William Le Queux had been commissioned by the *Daily Mail* to produce a book supporting its campaign to strengthen the British Army. The result, *The Invasion of 1910*, was a worldwide success, selling over 1 million copies before being translated into twenty-seven languages and even made into a film released in October 1914. The story told of a German invasion of Britain via Goole and the Humber, and Sheffield played an important part:

ENGLISHMEN !
Your Homes are Desecrated !
Your Children are Starving !
Your Loved Ones are Dead !
WILL YOU REMAIN IN COWARDLY INACTIVITY?

The German Eagle flies over London. Hull, Newcastle and Birmingham are in ruins. Manchester is a German City. Norfolk, Essex, and Suffolk form a German colony. The Kaiser's troops have brought death, ruin, and starvation upon you.

WILL YOU BECOME GERMANS?

NO !

Join THE DEFENDERS and fight for England. You have England's Millions beside you.

LET US RISE !

Let us drive back the Kaiser's men.
Let us shoot them at sight.
Let us exterminate every single man who has desecrated English soil.
Join the New League of Defenders.
Fight for your homes. Fight for your wives. Fight for England.

FIGHT FOR YOUR KING !

The National League of Defenders' Head Offices.
Bristol, September 21st, 1910.

A call to arms for a defeated Britain. From William Le Queux's Invasion of 1910.

The town of Sheffield throughout Tuesday and Wednesday was the scene of the greatest activity. Day and night the streets were filled with an excited populace, and hour by hour the terror increased ...

Every train arriving from the North was crowded with Volunteers and troops of the line from all stations in the Northern Command ... These troops, with their ambulances, their baggage, and all their impedimenta, created the utmost confusion at both railway stations. The great concourse of idlers cheered and cheered again, the utmost enthusiasm being displayed when each battalion forming up was marched away out of the town to the position chosen for the defence, which now reached from Woodhouse on the south, overlooking and commanding the whole valley of the river Rother, through Catcliffe, Brinsworth, and Tinsley, previously alluded to, skirting Greasborough to the high ground north of Wentworth, also commanding the river Don and all approaches to it through Mexborough, and over the various bridges which spanned this stream -- a total of about eight miles.

The south flank was thrown back another four miles to Norton, in an endeavour to prevent the whole position being turned, should the Germans elect to deliver their threatened blow from a more southerly point than was anticipated.

The total line, then, to be occupied by the defenders was about twelve miles, and into this front was crowded the heterogeneous mass of troops of all arms. The post of honour was at Catcliffe, the dominating key to the whole position, which was occupied by the sturdy soldiers of the 1st Battalion West Riding Regiment and the 2nd Battalion Yorkshire Light Infantry, while commanding every bridge crossing the rivers which lay between Sheffield and the invaders were concentrated the guns of the 7th Brigade Royal Horse Artillery, and of the Field Artillery, the 2nd, the 30th, the 37th, and 38th Brigades, the latter having hurriedly arrived from Bradford.

All along the crests of these slopes which formed the defence of Sheffield, rising steeply from the river at times up to five hundred feet, were assembled the Volunteers, all now by daybreak on Thursday morning busily engaged in throwing up shelter-trenches and making hasty earthwork defences for the guns. The superintendence of this force had merged itself into that of the Northern Command, which nominally had its headquarters in York, but which had now been transferred to Sheffield itself, for the best of reasons – that it was of no value at York, and was badly wanted farther south. General Sir George Woolmer, who so distinguished himself in South Africa, had therefore shifted his headquarters to the Town Hall in Sheffield, but as soon as he had begun to get the line of defence completed, he, with his staff, moved on to Handsworth, which was centrally situated.

In the command were to be found roughly twenty-three battalions of Militia and forty-eight of Volunteers; but, owing to the supineness and neglect of the Government, the former regiments now found themselves, at the moment when wanted, greatly denuded of officers, and, owing to any lack of encouragement to enlist, largely depleted in men. As regards the Volunteers, matters were even worse, only about fifteen thousand having responded to the call to arms. And upon these heroic men, utterly insufficient in point of numbers, Sheffield had to rely for its defence.

Away to the eastward of Sheffield – exactly where was yet unknown – sixty thousand perfectly equipped and thoroughly trained German horse, foot, and artillery, were ready at any moment to advance westward into our manufacturing districts!

The Invasion of 1910 was just one of a raft of similar books, stories, plays and films based on the belief that Germany would one day attempt to invade Britain. So strong was the belief that in 1913 a recruiting drive for the South Yorkshire Territorial Forces told audiences that German Zeppelin airships could, and probably would, be used to land an attacking force anywhere in the country at any time. Even as war broke out, stories of a naval battle in the North Sea spread like wildfire, raising fears that the invasion was already on its way. Reactions to the outbreak of war were mixed. Even in London, where tourists in town for the Bank Holiday heard the news after a day in the pub, the cheering crowds on one side of Trafalgar Square were matched by an anti-war demonstration on the other. There was no rejoicing in Sheffield, however; only a calm acceptance that there was no going back.

Mobilisation began immediately. Glossop Road baths were taken over as offices for the military to process reservists returning to their units and the Army Recruiting office on St George's Terrace found around 200 men per day turning up to answer Lord Kitchener's call for men aged between 19 and 30 to enlist. Soon, other offices sprang up in Attercliffe, Brightside, Heeley and East Parade and the university held parades daily for recruits to the Special Reserve of Officers and the Territorial Force. By 12 August, the age limit was raised to 42 and men who had already been turned away were encouraged to try again. Appeals appeared almost daily for men with special skills: Colonel Bingham's request for motorcyclists to join the Sheffield-based 1/1st West Riding Engineers brought dozens of responses and the positions were filled in a single day. Others joined the local Territorial Force – the York and Lancaster Regiment, Queen's Own Yorkshire Dragoons and the West Riding Artillery

Gavrilo Princip (centre), captured after shooting Archduke Franz Ferdinand in Sarajevo.

Territorials of the Hallamshires mobilise in August 1914.

Queues outside recruiting offices across the country saw men waiting hours for the chance to enlist.

and Medical Corps units based in the city. Although recruiting was brisk and Kitchener soon got the first 100,000 men of his planned 'New Army', more were still needed. By early September, it was claimed that Sheffield recruiting offices were unable to cope with demand as men queued for eight or nine hours for their turn before some gave up in disgust and went home. In an attempt to improve matters, the disused skating rink of 'The Jungle' on Hawley Street was taken over, as was the Corn Exchange building, and extra doctors were drafted in to speed up the process of medical examination. Between August and the end of September, up to 10,000 men were reported to have made the trip to the recruiting offices – about 10 per cent of the city's male workforce at the time.

CIVILIAN VOLUNTEERS

Sir,

If this war continues for, say six months, at the end of two or three the country will want some more men, and will only have untrained ones to draw from. Would it not be rather a good idea to start a training centre in Sheffield for a body of men, a kind of Citizen Army. There are many who, owing to various ties, will not volunteer at present, but who, if things got more serious, would certainly put everything aside and place themselves at the service of the country. If these men could now receive some training the country would in case of need have a useful disciplined body of men to draw from. I am writing to you as I think that through the medium of your paper some scheme of the sort might be started.

Yours etc 'SPERO' Sheffield August 11 1914

Evening Telegraph, 13 August 1914

Within days, a new army of civilian volunteers was created and by the end of 1914, Sheffield had over 4,000 men and women who gave up their free time to learn military skills (and paid for the privilege from their own pockets) so that they could assist the army in case of invasion. Initially resisted by the War Office, the Volunteer Training Corps became the model for the Home Guard of the Second World War.

Recruiting speech, c. 1914–15.

The decision to enlist, though, was not an easy one. Army pay was notoriously poor and with food prices rising every day, men with families simply could not afford the cut in income that joining up would bring. With a collier earning at least 8*s* a day, the drop to just 1*s* a day as a soldier was a serious problem. Even the additional pay for skilled men and the separation allowance paid for families rarely made up the shortfall and so some employers offered a deal: any employee voluntarily enlisting would be put on half pay and have a job waiting for them on their return. Even this, though, could mean real hardship for some families if the breadwinner enlisted.

Young men came under increasing pressure to join up and by 1915, 'volunteers' were often men who felt blackmailed into enlisting.

In class-conscious Edwardian society, service as an ordinary soldier in the army was not regarded as the right sort of environment for respectable young men, so in September 1914 Lord Derby proposed forming a new sort of unit using men from the same walks of life, creating a 'Stockbroker's Battalion' as an example of what could be done. Soon, others were following suit in an effort to create battalions in which a man could serve alongside what newspapers referred to as 'the right sort of comrade' and within days dozens of new units with titles like 'Post Office Rifles', 'Civil Service Rifles' and even 'the City of Glasgow Corporation Tramways Battalion' were being formed. Herbert Fisher, Vice Chancellor of Sheffield University, was approached by students about raising a unit. Fisher took up the idea and gained support from the Chancellor, the Mayor and the Duke of Norfolk, who in turn contacted the War Office for permission to recruit a battalion of men from the 'professional classes' of the city. On 10 September, recruiting began for the Sheffield University and City Special Battalion of the York and Lancaster Regiment.

REFUGEES
Around 3,000 Belgian civilians and wounded soldiers were brought to Sheffield in 1914 and cared for by donations from the people of the city. In 1921 a monument was raised in City Road cemetery to commemorate forty-four refugees who did not live to see their homeland again.

Richard Sparling, sports editor of the *Sheffield Telegraph*, was one of those enlisting and later recalled his fellow recruits as '£500 a year business men, stockbrokers, engineers, chemists, metallurgical experts, University and public school men, medical students, journalists, schoolmasters, craftsmen, shop assistants, secretaries, and all sorts of clerks'. J.R. 'Reg' Glenn was another early volunteer:

I worked for the Sheffield Education Department. My friend Ned Muxlow who worked in the same office as me came in and said, 'Shall we go and enlist in the City Battalion?' I said 'Alright, we can go at dinner time' but he replied 'no, let's go now'. So I got my cap and went and signed on. Instead of getting the King's shilling we received 1/6d. I don't know why and it's worried me ever since. I still spent it though!

Sheffield City Battalion on parade at Brammall Lane.

Learning military drill. Many volunteers came from youth organisations and already knew the basics. Often they were promoted on that basis alone.

Volunteers being sworn in. Next came the presentation of the King's shilling – their first day's wage.

Afterwards, Reg and Ned went back to their office to finish the day. In later life he was asked why he had enlisted:

> I don't know so much ... people talk about fighting for your King and country but I don't think there was so much of that about us. It was excitement. It was our pals were joining up and it was the thing to do and when you've been in an office for some years you feel you want a change and probably the excitement and the thoughts of going travelling around and a different kind of life probably had a lot to do with it. I dare say ... patriotism had something to do with it. It must have because we all have that inside of us but I think a lot of it was the excitement of going and doing something else ...

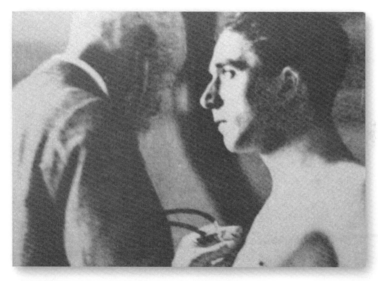

A recruit is examined. Some volunteers in the early days slipped through without even the most basic medical, allowing underage boys to join the army.

Men of the Sheffield City Battalion parade for the first time.

It was a feeling shared by F.B. Vaughan, another early recruit:

I said to the boss, 'I want to join the Army, I want to be released from my job'. So he said to me, 'Here in the steel-works you are doing just as much for your country just as much for the nation, as though you were in the Army.' Well, I couldn't see myself catching the 8.40 to Brightside every morning and leaving for home in the afternoon, doing all the little jobs in the evening, and all the time my pals were suffering – probably dying somewhere – they were serving their country. I couldn't see myself carrying on in that particular way, so I said, 'I'm awfully sorry but I have made up my mind, I must go.' And he saw that I was deter-mined and he said, 'Well then, go to the wages office and they will pay you whatever is due to you. But we shall not save your job for you when you come back and we shall not pay you anything while you are away.' I said, 'All right, I accept those conditions.' My mind was made up, the die was cast, and when I finally joined the Sheffield Battalion, as 256, Private F. B. Vaughan, Sheffield Battalion York and Lancasters – all at a bob a day – you know I was a very

Until uniforms arrived, the Pals wore their own clothes for training.

happy man. It was not just a sudden decision that I made to join the Army. My pals were going, chaps I had kicked about with in the street, kicking tin cans or a football, and chaps I knew very well in the city. And then if you looked in the newspapers we saw that Canadians were coming, Australians were coming, South Africans were coming – they were catching the first available boat to England to get there before the war was over. Then when you went to the pictures you'd be shown crowds of young men drilling in Hyde Park or crowding round the recruiting office, or it might be a band playing 'Tipperary'. The whole thing was exciting, and even in the pulpits – although it started rather shakily at first – they eventually decided to come down on the side of the angels and blessed our little mission. I don't know whether patriotism entered into it or not, possibly so. We were stirred, I know, by the atrocities, or the alleged atrocities, when the Germans invaded Belgium and France. The other great factor was that the womenfolk, fifty per cent of the population, were very keen on the war. Before long they were wearing regimental badges, regimental buttons, little favours in their hats or coats, and they were offering to do the jobs men had done in civil life, so that men could be released. Some of them would stop us in the street and say, 'Well, why aren't you in khaki?' In other words the whole effect was cumulative, but we were not pressed, we made our own decisions.

Leaving behind his £5-a-week job, Reg Glenn joined his new mates learning military drill dressed in their own clothes at Bramall Lane until the club's directors complained about the damage to their turf. In December, the battalion marched out of town to their new home at Redmires Camp. By then, civilian suits had been replaced not by khaki, but by Post Office blue serge uniforms – the only material available. Even if a uniform at least helped them feel more part of something, it sometimes gave off the wrong message. Men walking out in Sheffield were asked if they were Belgian soldiers whilst Herbert Hall recalled:

The battalion was on a route march one day and was passing through the village of Bamford in Derbyshire. Two old ladies were standing at the side of the road watching us go by. One was overheard to say to the other, 'Ee, it must be a terrible war if they have to turn out convicts to fight in it!'

For some, the Sheffield Pals were yet another sign of the class divide in the city and letters appeared complaining that ordinary working men were excluded. Years of poor diet and harsh living conditions had left many from the poorer areas suffering health problems that meant they failed to meet the height requirement (eventually dropped to just 5ft), others had serious dental problems (which would affect their ability to eat the hard tack biscuits that formed the army's iron rations). Something as simple as a speech impediment could be cause for rejection. Left at home to face the constant reminders that they should be serving, they looked for something they could do to help.

Sending 'convicts' to fight. Short of uniforms, the City Battalion were issued Post Office blue attire, which some bystanders mistook for prison uniforms.

Local civilian militias were started all over the country. Sheffield's defenders were taught to use weapons by the local rifle club.

The Volunteer Training Corps struggled to gain acceptance by the military authorities.

In the years before the war, the threat of civil war over the issue of Home Rule for Ireland had been widely reported, and with it the formation of an army of civilians – the Ulster Volunteer Force – ready to do battle against the fighters of the Irish Republican movement. There had also been the rapid growth of the Boy Scout movement, designed as it was to be a grassroots organisation in which anyone interested could start their own group using the guidance provided by Baden-Powell's bestselling book. Together, the two provided a model for paramilitary organisations that sprang up in towns and cities around Britain.

Sir Percy Harris noted:

On August 5th, 1914, I suggested in a letter to *The Times* 'the forming in the parks of evening camps on the lines of the Irish Nationalist and Ulster Volunteers.' Next morning my letter-box was crammed with offers of service from all over the country. A meeting followed, when Lord Desborough was elected president and myself honorary secretary. The movement spread, and units started training up and down the country. It grew to such proportions that the War Office got alarmed and issued an order prohibiting any kind of volunteer training. However, my committee had promises of vast sums of money to train and equip units. It seemed a pity to throw away this enthusiasm. As a result of a talk with the then Under-Secretary for War, I was authorised to keep the committee together for future possible action, but there did not then seem much possibility of our services being required. In November, the unexpected did happen. There was talk of possible raids to demoralise the civil population. Lord Kitchener therefore told Lord Desborough that the Army Council had decided to authorise our committee to organise training corps which, in the last resort, could be used for home defence. The conditions were stringent. First, only those were to be registered who were 'not eligible through age to serve in the Regular or Territorial Army, or are unable to do so for some genuine reason to be recorded in the Corps Register, and in the case of the latter, they must agree in writing to enlist if specially called upon to do so.' Those were the days of voluntary enlistment. Lord Kitchener was anxious that this volunteer force should not interfere with his great recruiting campaign. Another stipulation was that 'No arms, ammunition or clothing will be supplied from public sources, nor will financial assistance be given.'

Men who, for various reasons, were unable to enlist soon formed themselves into 'town guards' to learn drill and weapons handling with a view to assisting the army if an invasion came. Technically illegal, and liable to be shot as terrorists by any invading army, once started the movement proved impossible to stop. Instead, Sheffield's enthusiastic amateurs were invited to train with the Sheffield Rifle Club and were formed into what would become known as the 4Cs – the Chief Constable's Civilian Corps.

Police special constables were recruited to replace police officers recalled to the army. Often given no training, they were used to guard 'vulnerable points'.

A route march to Redmires took place on Sunday, 27 September 1914. For many years, Sheffield had been the home of 'The Jungle', a combination zoo and fairground founded by Frank Bostock and housed in an area near the city centre where slum clearances had left a large open space, and this is where training commenced at 8 p.m. the next evening. Over the coming weeks membership grew until by the end of October over 4,000 men paraded for an inspection by

LAW AND DORA
Between 4 August 1914 and 31 March 1920, 800 British civilians were tried by military courts martial.

the Lord Mayor. The fact that he was almost an hour late and no press attended left many feeling disgruntled and complaining that they were seen as merely 'inferior policemen'. Reluctant to acknowledge them at first, the War Office eventually gave in to demands and began organising the 'Volunteer Training Corps' on military lines, their uniform limited to a red armband with the letters 'GR' (Georgius Rex) emblazoned on it to signify that the man was on government duty. The age and physical condition of many of the 'Methusiliers' led some to speculate that it stood for 'God's Rejects' or, more often, 'Gorgeous Wrecks'. To make matters worse, after working to rid themselves of the perception that they were second-rate special constables, one furious

One of the 'Gorgeous Wrecks' on duty.

volunteer wrote to the local paper complaining that a police constable had looked at the man's smart new armband and asked if he were 'an auxiliary postman'.

By March 1915, the 4Cs had been incorporated into the Volunteer Training Corps and had expanded to include cyclists, to act as scouts, and even a women's section, whose members argued (unsuccessfully) their need to be armed. By then, a full set of rules had been issued, laying out permitted uniforms (a grey/ green serge tunic cut to fit over a cardigan) and rank structures. Commanders were to be permitted to carry swords only if their whole unit had rifles – but by 1916 there were 12,000 volunteers in the West Riding with only 750 rifles between them. Most paraded and guarded their posts with wooden dummy rifles bought from a London dealer for 10s each. Motor Volunteer car owners provided

> Under the terms of DORA, a man buying a glass of sherry for his wife could face the same sentence – six months' imprisonment or £100 fine – as someone selling cocaine.

Volunteer Training Corps uniforms.

PRIVATE.
(Original Pattern.)

OFFICER.
(The Rank Mark is that of a Company Commander.)

PRIVATE.
(Permissible Alternative Style.)

UNIFORMS.

essential transport to move wounded troops to and from local hospitals and frequently provided a free taxi service to soldiers from outlying areas whose already short leave from the front would have been even shorter had they been forced to wait for the next available public transport after the long overnight journey from France.

Sir Percy wrote in *The Spectator* of September 1939:

> The question naturally arises, was the force of any use? The answer is emphatically 'Yes'. In the crisis of March, 1918, when the Allies were in full retreat, the call came to send overseas every available man. I remember attending a conference at the War Office to discuss how far it was safe to rely on the Volunteer Force for Home Defence. The experts agreed that by this time the force was so efficient that for all practical purposes home defence could be left to the Volunteers. The result was it was possible to denude the country of troops. The force more or less continued a part-time force very much like the Territorials in peace time. But they were available and could be embodied for Home Defence at short notice. They did actually take over much defence work, such as coast patrol, searchlight work, digging trenches, miles of which were constructed in the London area at week-ends. Besides, hundreds of thousands of men passed through its ranks in the early days of the War and entered the regular Army as trained men instead of as raw recruits.

Six months after the article appeared the Gorgeous Wrecks were back, this time as the 'Dad's Army' of the Home Guard.

Even as the volunteers began training, rumours flew around of German agents travelling the country to sabotage railway lines and other important sites. With so few men available to guard them, the task fell instead to enthusiastic volunteers from the Boy Scouts who mounted guard on reservoirs, railways and other potentially vulnerable points.

Former Scout H. Middleton of Attercliffe, writing in 1981, recalled:

DUMMY RIFLES FOR DRILL
From **12/6** to **48/-** per dozen.

SHORT LEE-ENFIELD MODEL
CORRECT BALANCE AND WEIGHT **45/-** per dozen.

Send for Sample and Lists : **SUMMERS, 28, CHEAPSIDE, LONDON.**

The Parade Drill Rifle.
AN EXACT COPY OF THE SHORT LEE - ENFIELD.

Correctly Weighted and Balanced, Bolt, Magazine and Trigger, Sights, Slings, Piling Swivel and Adjustable Strap, &c.

As used by Home Defence Leagues for route marching.

10/6 each. Special Prices for Quantities.

On view Central Association | Sole Agents: **TEPSON & CO.,** | Manufacturers: **GEMS & GRABHAM,**
Volunteer Training Corps. | 28, Essex Street, Strand. | Lancaster Road, North Kensington.

There was a scare that the dams were going to be poisoned, and members of the Pitsmoor group were for some weeks, at the beginning of the war, on duty all nights at a reservoir at High Green. Permanent camps were established at Rivelin, Redmires and Bradfield I think it was. Scouts were for weeks out there day and night. Boys who had left school and weren't working were there all the time. They were organised by the central authorities in Sheffield and on the suggestion of the police.

Short of weapons, the volunteers had to rely on dummy rifles.

By the end of 1914, 100,000 Scouts across the country were involved in the war effort, working night and day. Edmund Priestman, leader of the 16th (Westbourne) Troop estimated that he travelled up to 80 miles a day on his rounds of the various Scout guards around Sheffield. In recognition of their important work, the government made it an offence for anyone not an official member of the Scout Movement to wear their uniform and a special 'War Service' badge was created for twenty-eight days' unpaid service, later increasing to at least fifty days. Scouts worked as unpaid orderlies in hospitals, helped refugees settle into their new homes and even acted as messengers in military bases and police stations. As the threat of enemy air raids grew, their work became potentially dangerous, as recalled by H. Middleton:

Scouts and Guides went away to camp, where they were employed on farms.

> … In case the telephone wires were brought down [in a raid], we were delegated in pairs and we had a beat and when the sirens went we used to go on this beat which was kind of relay, you see. Now my beat was from Bawtry Road … to Tinsley Terminus and there we were met by two other scouts that had a beat from there to a relay until it went to the police station … that was a right job, getting out of bed at one o'clock in the morning, go walking up and down there … we did that as part of a badge that was awarded – the War Service Badge.

By 1916, the Ministry of National Service began to arrange Scout camps in areas where help was needed in the fields. In 1917, Middleton was sent to a camp near Holbeach for a fortnight over summer, working six hours a day to help with the flax harvest and earning '25 shillings a week we got at the time for the flax and we used to have to pull it up by the roots'. Other Scouts had been taken on for other roles. According to the *Sheffield Yearbook and Record* of 1917:

Scouts from Sheffield were sent to help gather the harvests, earning up to 25s a week.

> In April 1917, when all available troops were required for foreign service, the Pitsmoor Troop were requested by the military authorities to supply a number of scouts to work with a reduced army team in the Parkwood anti-aircraft gun site. Nine boys signed on, seven for work on the gun and two for the searchlight. These scouts attended three drills per week and soon became proficient in the duties assigned to them and on May 25 the volunteer detachment was ordered to Spurn Head along with the regular team for a shooting trial. The scout team fired very successfully the rounds allocated to them and were specially commended by the inspecting officer.

As the war progressed, Scouts became an important part of local defence. Buglers were driven around in cars to sound the alert and 'all clear' during air raids.

Men of the York and Lancaster Transport Battalion unload food supplies. Docks battalions like this were paid union rates as well as army wages when working in the UK.

As the men left for the war, women came forward to take their places at work. From genteel ladies gathering in parlours to knit socks to nurses serving within range of the German guns on the Western Front, the war gave women the chance to break down opposition from employers as they fought for their right to join the war effort and they soon proved themselves capable of working in engineering, in agriculture as part of the Women's Land Army formed in 1917, on tramways, as drivers and even, for the first time, as university lecturers. When an explosion ripped through Room 42 of the Barnbow Munitions Factory in Leeds, killing thirty-five 'munitionettes' outright and maiming many more, work stopped only long enough to clear the bodies. That same night, teenage girls determined to keep the men at the front supplied went back to work in Room 42 with blood still staining the floor. No record exists of the number of women poisoned by the toxic chemicals used in munitions work but many individual cases exist, and certainly many were killed or seriously injured in accidents caused by working hours that were long and hard. In April 1915, Sheffield MP William Anderson raised the issue in Parliament:

Street shrines sprang up in local communities to remember men of the area, especially after the Somme.

Munitionettes.

[Can I ask] the Secretary of State for the Home Department whether his attention has been drawn to the legal prosecution of a firm of engineers engaged at cartridge-making in Armley, Leeds, in which it was shown that a girl under eighteen years of age worked from 6 a.m. on Friday till 7 a.m. on Saturday, when she met with an accident, whilst an older woman worked from 6 a.m. on Friday till 11 a.m. on Saturday; whether he is aware that the Stipendiary Magistrate declined to convict on the ground that he might be limiting the output of ammunition; whether his attention has also been drawn to the death from exhaustion of an artificer at the Small Arms Factory, Enfield, who was stated to have worked eighty and a-half hours a week since August, thirty-two hours a week above normal; and whether he can take steps in co-operation with the military and naval authorities to encourage only such industrial conditions as will not destroy physical health and in the end retard output?

By the end of 1914, Sheffield, 'armourer to the empire', reported that only around 1,000 people were unemployed from a population of 454,000 as the city prepared to play its part.

3

'TEN ACRES OF HELL ...'

As the initial shock of being at war wore off, Sheffield businesses soon found trade picking up. In 1914 the city was home to the world's leading producers of armour plate, gun barrels and heavy ammunition and had made heavy investments in research and development that had led, in part, to the creation of stainless steel in 1913. Naval contracts alone were so large that generations of Sheffielders referred to the area around Janson Street as 't' Admiralty' because of the Engineers' Office and Inspection Office set up to oversee Royal Navy contracts in the city. In 1914, the male workforce was over 100,000, 70 per cent of whom would remain at work throughout the war, with some having joined the army but then sent back to

'Ten acres of hell'. Sheffield's armaments factories expanded enormously during the war. This is the River Don Works in 1919.

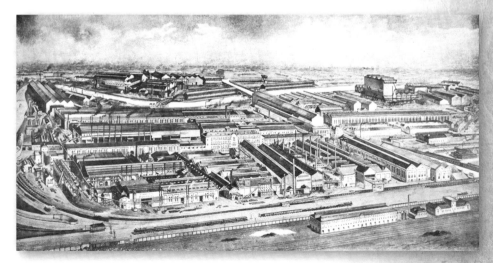

*Shrapnel shell
workshop.*

*Preparing shells
for filling.*

work at their old jobs. By December, an estimated 75 per cent of Sheffield businesses were involved in some form of war work – but there were problems.

In September 1914, the *Sheffield Telegraph* had reported that the rapid expansion of the army had created a new market for local cutlers: 'The firms who are not participating in the boom are exceptional, as anyone can dispose of the whole of their stocks of a suitable pattern.' But by early 1915, demand had outstripped supply and Sheffield's Master Cutler issued an appeal to other towns and cities for donations of razors from patriotic citizens:

The *Bradford Weekly Telegraph* of 19 February noted:

> Sending razors to Sheffield, savours of the adage about carrying coals to Newcastle. But it seems that Sheffield is wanting razors very badly ... The demand upon Sheffield has been so great for army purposes that the city cannot supply them all, and as the English soldiers are so particular about their toilet, it is necessary that an outside appeal should be made.

Rudder frames for HMS Australia *being transported across the Pennines to Salford for shipping to Clydebank, 1918. Despite being landlocked, Sheffield was an important centre for naval construction.*

The razors would, it continued, 'be sent as a gift for the troops'. Despite trying to adapt by turning to the manufacture of swords,

Thousands of men were released by the army to return to their old jobs because of the shortage of specialist workers.

surgical instruments, kitchen utensils and even flechettes ('little arrows' – sharpened steel darts dropped from aircraft), Sheffield's 1,600 cutlers found work drying up. They had relied too heavily on traditional, high-quality techniques and soon found themselves losing out to mass-produced American imports.

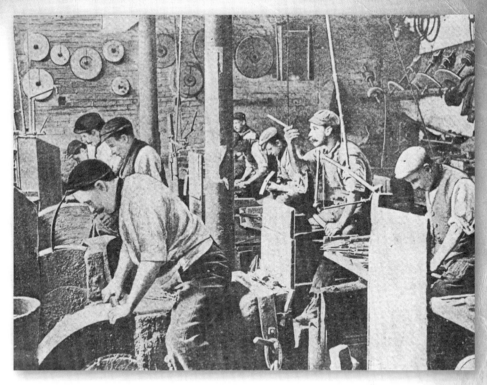

If the cutlers were having a hard time, the same could not be said of the arms manufacturers where the scale of the expansion of both the army and the armament industry was enormous. Vickers held a contract to supply 287 machine guns in 1914 but by 1918, the number had risen to 120,864. In the first eight weeks of war, panic buying by the War Office had meant the 192 artillery guns actually on order had been increased to 1,792 in three separate orders, to which the French Government added a further order for fifty guns per week. With no co-ordinating body, no company could cope with such huge orders and arms production fell far short of demand – only 1,022 of the 2,338 guns expected from various companies were delivered by the

Cutlery grinding. Sheffield's cutlers were geared towards quality rather than quantity and soon found they were unable to keep up with demand.

SHELL OUTPUT FOR THE COMMONLY USED 18-POUNDER FIELD GUN		
Shell	High Explosive	Shrapnel
1914	9,110	341,700
1915	978,600	4,252,000
1916	11,872,568	22,519,021
1917	20,609,010	27,445,226
1918	14,318,178	18,422,811
Total	47,787,486	72,980,758

(*Statistics of the Military Effort of the British Empire in the Great War* (HMSO 1922))

After fighting for the right to vote, suffragists and suffragettes also had to fight for their right to help the war effort.

July 1915 deadline. Only about a third of the promised ammunition had been supplied.

In France, as in Britain, the enthusiastic recruiting of 1914 had had an unforeseen consequence. Thousands of volunteers had come forward from industries vital to the war effort, leaving mining and steel production in particular undermanned and leading to a slump in production. The River Don Works alone claimed to have lost almost 1,000 men and so great was the problem that, following the Admiralty's lead, large firms began issuing War Service badges to their employees to help guard against the attentions of the recruiters and the young women who had taken to handing out white feathers to any man they regarded as shirking his duty by not being in uniform (and even sometimes to men invalided out of the forces by their wounds).

CAPITAL ISSUED TO SHAREHOLDERS OF SHEFFIELD COMPANIES		
	1914	1919
Vickers	£7,015,000	£20,663,237
John Brown	£3,573,000	£4,187,500
Cammell-Laird	£2,372,895	£4,018,416
Hadfield's	£700,000	£1,900,000
Thomas Firth	£520,000	£1,600,000

COMRADES OF THE GREAT WAR
(SHEFFIELD BRANCH).
REGISTERED UNDER THE WAR CHARITIES ACT, 1916.

"LEST WE FORGET."

THE FLAG DAY OF THE YEAR

WILL BE HELD ON

SATURDAY, AUGUST 3rd, 1918.

BUY A FLAG to alleviate the sufferings of those who "WATCH and WAIT."

"LOOK AFTER THE WIFE AND KIDDIES, MATEY."

Sample of letter received :—" Please accept my sincere thanks for the grant of 10/- per week your Committee have made to me. Owing to bad health and worry in connection with the bad news from the War Office in respect to my husband, I really don't know what my children and I would have done had it not been for your kind advice and help."

Donations will be gratefully acknowledged by the Hon. Treasurer, C. A. ELLIOTT, Esq., Hallam Gate Road, Sheffield.
W. J. HORNE, Hon. Secretary, Flag Day Committee.
Comrades of the Great War, 63, Pond Street.

WE, THE "COMRADES," SOLICIT YOUR HELP TO DO THIS.

By early 1915, generals were already complaining of the shortage of artillery rounds and the 'Shell Scandal' forced the creation of a new Ministry of Munitions to oversee production. Around 40,000 skilled men were released from the military back to their old jobs, some still wearing uniform as they started back to work, but there was still a shortage of labour that could only be alleviated by taking on semi-skilled and unskilled workers. Unions, concerned about the dilution of the labour force and the potential impact on wages at the end of the war, resisted initially but eventually recognised that concessions had to be made. Women and men unfit for military service began to enter the workplace in such numbers that new temporary accommodation hostels, houses and 'colony blocks' had to be built around the larger factories to accommodate thousands of new workers coming to the city. Many more were billeted in private homes. Special transport had to be laid on to enable workers to get into the factories from outlying areas but most of the new buildings were concentrated around Wincobank and Tinsley, some of which were converted into council homes after the war.

Charity 'flag days' became a feature of everyday life, raising money for foreign aid, refugees or, as here, to support the dependents of men serving in the forces.

COST OF ARTILLERY BARRAGES
Arras (25 March–8 April 1917)
Rounds fired 2,687,653
Cost £13,162,689 – 13s 8d

Messines (26 May–6 June 1917)
Rounds fired 3,561,530
Cost £17,505,453 – 18s 8d

Ypres (17–30 July 1917)
Rounds fired 4,283,550
Cost £22,211,380 – 14s 4d

(*Statistics of the Military Effort of the British Empire in the Great War* (HMSO 1922)

Battle Bowlers

When the British troops arrived in France in 1914, they wore peaked woollen 'Service Dress' cap. French troops wore a leather peaked 'Kepi' and the Germans the famous 'Pickelhaube' spiked helmet made of leather. None offered any real protection and, as the two sides dug in and settled into the trench stalemate that was to mark the Western Front, the number of head injuries soared.

Legend has it that the French general August-Louis Adrian one day encountered a soldier whose life had been saved by his habit of placing his metal food bowl under his kepi, where it had deflected a German bullet. Whatever the true story, by 1915 the French Army had begun to issue the Adrian helmet to its troops, dramatically reducing the numbers killed by shrapnel shells exploding over the trenches and showering lethal fragments onto the men below. Letters began appearing in the British press demanding that troops be given some sort of similar protection. Initially, stores of Adrian helmets were supplied to front-line trenches as 'trench supplies' to be handed over between units as they rotated through their tours of duty until a more permanent solution could be found.

A number of British designs were put forward. John Leopold Brodie's offered several advantages over the French model. It was constructed so that it could be pressed from a single thick sheet of steel, giving it added strength and making it easier to produce. Brodie's design had a shallow circular crown with a wide brim around the edge to protect the wearer's head and shoulders from shrapnel projectiles bursting above the trenches and came with a leather liner and chinstrap. The original (Type A) had barely gone into production before Sir Robert Hadfield of Sheffield suggested that his patented steel, mixed with 12 per cent manganese, would produce a stronger version that could withstand a .45 bullet fired from just 10ft away.

Hadfield's researchers approached Dixons of Sheffield, a silversmiths and cutlers, for help in developing the stamps needed to produce a prototype. Dixons turned to their existing stock and found a soup bowl die that, with minor modifications, could be used. The iconic 'soup plate' pattern went into production by the end of 1915 and over 7 million would be produced by twenty sheet mills in the Sheffield area for use by British and Commonwealth troops. The 'tin hat' was born.

Comparison shot of British (left) and German (right).

*Munitionettes
at Thomas
Firth & Sons,
December 1918.*

In July 1914, there were an estimated 212,000 women working in the munitions industry in Britain: by 1918 the number was almost 920,000, with Thomas Firth & Sons employing over 5,000 at its Templeborough plant alone. Vickers employed around 16,000 and workers were drafted in from all over the country. Among those joining the workforce was artist and designer Septimus Bennett, originally from Stoke-on-Trent but working at a studio in London when war broke out. In 1915 he attempted to enlist but was rejected and so decided to work in munitions instead. He made his way to Sheffield:

Just one glance at this district is enough to put anyone off the idea of Munitions. It is absolutely forbidding. Belching furnaces, the rumbling noises of hidden machinery, the hissing of steam jets over black pools of water, the vast prison-like places employing seven, eight and ten thousand hands – make me shudder to think of having to work amongst such surroundings, not to mention living. There are rows of houses in mean streets, but it would be quite impossible to live in such …

June 29th
I start at Vickers, Holme Lane, at 9am.
I knew the works yard well enough by sight, but the hidden mysteries behind a pair of unpainted double doors, through which I had seen men go to & fro had yet to be introduced to me.

   Once inside, the first impression was bewildering, for I hated machinery & the noise of same I thought it impossible to work in. I couldn't even hear what people said. The timekeeper took me to the foreman who took not the slightest notice of me for some time & I stood waiting & watching all these men each at work on a lathe about ten times the size of those I had seen at the university & apparently totally different. Eventually, the foreman a man named George Marsden came along again & I took a strong dislike to him straight away. He put me on to a great ugly lathe which looked to be very old & instructed someone to set me going.

Gradually, Septimus came to be accepted by his co-workers and would later look back on his time in Sheffield as having been worthwhile but, like many, the introduction to the world of the vast munitions works seemed to him to be like entering 'ten acres of hell'. The work paid well but brought with it long hours of repetitive work, the constant danger of accidents and explosions and exposure to the effects of picric acid, a yellow chemical used in dyeworks but also a vital component of the 'Lyddite' explosives used to fill the shells. Over time, skin and eyes took on a jaundiced look that earned munitions workers the nickname 'canaries' as the chemicals built up to lethal levels in the body.

Making shell cases.

Workers came to Sheffield from all over the world. The grave of an Australian munitions worker, Burngreave Cemetery. (Beth Lynch)

Whilst munitions work was vital, those conscientious objectors taking an 'absolutist' stance argued that in effect any job helped the war effort. The introduction of conscription in January 1916 had made every able-bodied man eligible for military service but allowed exemptions to be made in cases where being called up would cause extreme hardship or where there was a moral or religious objection to joining the military. Where men could show strong anti-war beliefs they would be offered jobs in other roles such as the 'Non Combatant Corps' working on the land, in forestry and so on. Most accepted these jobs but some argued that taking jobs as, for example, a bus conductor or postman helped the war effort by releasing another man to serve. One man, turned down for exemption and sent to work at a remount depot where horses were made ready for work in the army, refused to clean out a horse's stall on the grounds that he considered it to be 'materially helping the war effort'. Against such an argument it was almost impossible to find any solution but to subject the men to the same army discipline that their serving peers had agreed to and imprison them.

By 1918, though, it seemed they had a point. Virtually everyone had a role to play in the war effort. In February 1917, the German Kaiser had announced: 'We will frighten the British flag off the face of the waters and starve the British people until they, who have refused peace, will kneel and plead for it.'

From the start of the war, the Royal Navy had been preventing any ships reaching German ports, refusing to allow food to get through a blockade that would last until 1919 and lead to an estimated 750,000 deaths from starvation in Germany itself. In response, the German Navy had declared the seas around Britain a war zone, allowing them to sink any vessels within the English Channel and around the coast of Britain and Ireland. Unable to cope against the might of the Royal Navy's surface fleet, Germany

Munitionettes at work.

Steel helmets in production. Over 7 million would be produced by the end of the war.

relied instead on its submarines – the U-boats. At first it was a piece-meal campaign with at times only four U-boats active around the UK, but the worldwide food shortage created by the bad harvest of 1916 was an opportunity, the German High Command believed, to starve Britain out of the war. With most of the country's wheat and much of its other foodstuffs coming from overseas, planners confidently predicted that if they could attack any shipping on the high seas, they could starve Britain into submission in five months. In just three months from October 1916 to January 1917, almost 1.5 million tons of shipping was lost to submarines.

Between February and June, U-boats sank shipping carrying over 85,000 tons of sugar which, when added to the losses of barley, meant a beer shortage that forced many pubs to close over Easter. Later, the *Sheffield Year Book* recorded May and June as a time of 'near famine' and by August, the council were considering plans to licence the sale of horsemeat, previously dismissed as a foreign food associated with the Belgian refugees. There were mixed feelings. Some argued that Belgians were the main market and since most were working, they could afford to buy beef. There was no need, they said, to cater for the tastes of temporary immigrants. Others pointed out that there was a risk of greedy traders attempting to pass cheap horsemeat off as beef. There were fears it would be a propaganda coup for Germany to report that Britain was reduced to eating horses but in September, two shops opened on Westbar to sell it and by November there were five horse butchers in the city.

With so much wheat coming from overseas, it was estimated that eight of every ten loaves were made with imported flour and bread became the focus of a major campaign to avoid waste to the point where feeding a slice to an animal became a criminal offence. When Mrs Hobson of No. 221 Nottingham Street died in 1918, her son William decided, apparently against his late mother's wishes, to throw what the court later called 'the usual party' after the funeral and asked his brother-in-law, Albert Kramer, a pork butcher at No. 63 Spital Street, to cater for it. The party ended and everyone went home. A week later, William and Albert were arrested and charged under the Defence of the Realm Act with wasting bread. The story emerged in court: William's sister, Sarah Day, lived a few doors away from her mother and had refused to attend the party. There was what was described as 'a lot of bad blood' between them and, a week after the party, Mrs Day had gone to her mother's old home and allegedly found a loaf of bread that had gone mouldy. She immediately reported this to Inspector Thomas Toye of

Food rationing leaflet.

Help to Win the War !

The average weekly consumption by each family of the three staple foods should not exceed per head :—

BREAD . . . 4lbs.

OR (but not in addition) 3lbs. Flour.

MEAT . . 2½lbs.

SUGAR . . ½lb.

REMEMBER !

Our Food costs not only money but the lives of our brave Seamen.

County War Savings Committee.

Walsh, Printer, Southgate, Sleaford.

the Food Control Committee, who visited the house and declared the loaf inedible and therefore wasted. It was enough to have both William and Albert arrested and potentially facing imprisonment but when the matter reached Sheffield police court in February, the case against Kramer was quickly dropped and the argument centred on whose bread it actually was. William insisted that when he left the house, he had looked around and there was no bread on the table. He also claimed that he did not know that his sister had a key. Unable to prove that Sarah had not placed the loaf in the house in order to get back at her brother, the magistrates gave up and dismissed the case but trials for food wasting and hoarding were increasingly common as neighbour jealously watched neighbour for signs that they had more than their fair share.

Goods might be available, but a common problem was how to transport them. Shortages of fuel had seen the first gas-powered taxis on Sheffield streets in 1917, where motor vehicles had already become an increasingly rare sight. Horses were equally rare as demands for army transport rose and private horses were requisitioned. For a time, trams were used at night for freight but the need remained for a reliable form of heavy transport. A novel solution to the problem was found by Thomas Ward's company, who turned to the fairs and circuses that tended to winter in The Jungle in Sheffield city centre. Among them William Sedgewick's travelling menagerie, from where, in 1916, Ward's were able to secure the services of an elephant named Lizzie. Stabled near the factory, Lizzie soon became a familiar sight around the streets of the city,

Food Economy Campaign.

SYLLABUS of a Course of LESSONS to be given by MISS M. FERGUSSON

(With the consent of the Kesteven Education Committee).

Subject of Lesson.	Illustrative Dishes.
1. Bread and Flour Ration. Flour and Flour Substitutes.	Rice bread. Porridge. Barley scones. Maize pudding.
2. Explanation of Meat Ration. Stewing. Pot Roast. Meatless days.	Sea pie. Boned and stuffed breast of mutton. Dried green peas & cheese. Flaked maize and cheese.
3. Pulse Foods. Cereals. Flourless Puddings & Sauces.	Baked beans. Lentil and vegetable pie. Golden pudding & sauce. Ground rice or sago pudding
4. Stock. Soup. Vegetables. Potato Substitutes.	Lentil and tomato soup. Barley broth. Savoury rice. Oatmeal pudding.

The Food Economy Campaign aimed to teach housewives how to cook with only basic ingredients.

sometimes accompanied by camels to help share the load and the phrase 'it's like Tommy Ward's elephant' (it's very heavy) entered the local dialect. She even drew the attention of farmer John Hopwood of Sandygate who advertised for an elephant of his own, offering a 'good opportunity for a willing beast to learn farming' and eventually negotiated a trial for Lizzie when her contract with Ward's ended.

As food supplies ran low, long queues began to form outside shops and often people stood in line without even knowing what they were queuing for – only that something in short supply might be available. Workers coming off night shifts often had to join long queues before they could go home to sleep and children were kept off school to stand in line holding a place for their mothers. Voluntary rationing was encouraged, with housewives advised on what was deemed to be a reasonable amount of food and classes made available to teach women how to make 'meat-free meals' and potato bread. With the fishing industry severely hampered by not only heavy winter storms but also U-boats and mines, fish prices soared and chip shop owners lobbied Parliament for help with the vital war work of providing cheap meals. Wealthier families were encouraged to make use of lobster and oysters to leave

Lizzie at work.

Inspired by Lizzie's example, others found work for unemployed circus elephants.

The Sheffield Jungle and other menageries released animals to help the war effort.

cheaper types of seafood for the poor. In late 1917, as millions struggled to find food, newspapers reported how sumptuous meals were available at top London hotels for anyone with the money to afford them.

To try to alleviate the problem, the government bought up land and turned it over to agriculture. Over 7 million acres of local parks, gardens and even road verges were dug up to grow food crops under the Cultivation of Lands Order. Allotments, previously seen as a harmless hobby for cranks, became highly prized as 1.5 million more became available. A new 'Women's Land Army' was formed and men seeking exemption from military service were offered the chance to work in 'Agricultural Companies' to provide labour on farms. Over 250,000 women, 84,000 men deemed unfit for service and 30,000 prisoners of war were put to work growing food to keep Britain fed. The Home Office gave local education authorities powers to suspend by-laws governing school attendance so that schoolchildren could be employed in helping harvest crops and to gather chestnuts (which could be processed to produce chemicals needed for explosives), fodder for horses and even sphagnum moss from the moors for use in packing wound dressings. At school, girls sewed sandbags and children entertained troops in local hospitals or went out on fundraising collection days. Everyone, it seemed, had a part to play, but the old pre-war industrial disputes had not gone away. Special 'munitions courts' were set up to try cases of absenteeism and bad behaviour in munitions factories and workers objected to this interference, especially on top of rising costs, food shortages and claims that people were profiteering from the war which all added to the atmosphere of industrial

Under the Cultivation of Land Order, any open land was turned over to growing food.

unrest that had marked the years before the war. Strikes became an increasingly common feature of Sheffield life.

According to Bill Moore:

People were starting to turn against the government and against the war. In my family, it was heartbreaking. My father had been killed. My mum had died just after I was born and I was brought up by my grandmother, my father's mother. She was devastated by my father's death. Her hair turned white in a couple of weeks. I remember watching her and my grandfather weeping, trying to console each other. And some of my uncles never came back from the war, either. That was what was happening to lots of families in Sheffield. They were exhausted and they were angry. I can only describe it as a dark cloud hanging over us. But Sheffield was a proud city that had fought for its rights, going back to the days of the French Revolution, and that's what it did again in the war. Many times the engineering factories were out on strike.

Munitions worker Septimus Bennett recorded in his diary for 10 May 1917 his apprehension at being promoted to chargehand over members of the Amalgamated Society of Engineers (ASE), who were in a national dispute after an engineer was called up. He wrote:

The strike is causing much unrest, discomfort, & ill feeling in civilian life & if it continues will prove disas-trous to our success in the war ... I am not inclined to side with strikes, but I must agree that the ASE has a distinct grievance & strong grounds for same. But blame is attributable to both sides.

The government was allowing the military to call up skilled workers who had previously been in protected occupations and replace them at work with 'dilutees' – men not fit for service who were paid at a lower rate. The unions argued that this meant poorer quality work and risked experienced men coming home after the war to low wages. Bennett agreed with the grievance but wondered if the ASE were more concerned with their own interests:

> The workings of the ASE, particularly as it is composed today, are so secret that it is difficult for an outsider to know how the matter stands. I have even heard members of the ASE say themselves; in fact some of them have said to me: 'I'm damned if I know what exactly we are out for and I'm certainly ashamed of being seen walking about the streets' … Moreover, quite a number of them can't afford to be out & say so openly and that they strongly object to the taunts they receive at any street corner, particularly from women & through no fault of their own, as they say. But in this I do not agree. If they belong to a Society they must adhere to its rules & risk the consequences.

Although Yorkshire as a whole remained a centre for militancy, a government snapshot of industrial action in January 1918 showed more strikers there than in Scotland (the second highest rate), Wales and Northern Ireland combined. Balancing the need to protect hard-won rights for workers against the effects on men in France of the shortages caused by strikes was always going to be hard. For families with men serving, the sight of fit men of military age earning high wages and striking for more was a source of anger. 'A Prayer to Lloyd George' expressed the feelings of many local people toward the ASE:

> Don't send me in the army George,
> I'm in the ASE.
> Take all the bloody labourers,
> But for God's sake don't take me.
> You want me for a soldier?
> Well that can never be –
> A man of my ability
> And in the ASE!

For three weeks, the ASE remained out on strike until, with production severely affected, they won the battle. As the number of strikes grew, there was a growing mood of confrontation between police and pickets in the city as union organiser Albert Sweeting recalled:

> One day I advised them all to bring a big, thick stick with them because some of the Cossacks [mounted police] had rushed us in Earl Marshall Road. I went to report these Cossacks to the Chief Constable, Major Hall-Dallwood. He said, 'Well, you tell me, Mr Sweeting, how it is that your men went out armed yesterday?' 'Is it really necessary to tell you?', I asked. 'Yes.' 'Well, don't you know that the best line of defence is to be prepared to attack?' They never attacked us again after that.

By 1918, though, even hard-line unions were prepared to accept the call up of union members who were habitually absent from work and miners voted against a negotiated peace, arguing that Germany must be defeated. Tired and hungry though they may have been, Sheffield's workforce were determined to see it through.

4

'WILL THERE BE ANY REPLY?'

Prisoners of war were allowed to receive parcels and letters from home. Bread was supplied by bakeries in Switzerland and 'flag days' raised funds to send out packages including jam, tobacco, soap and various other 'comforts'.

By 1918, over 12 million letters and 1 million parcels each week were being delivered to soldiers overseas, where it was said that a letter to France reached its destination faster than one to another part of England. Even men imprisoned in prisoner-of-war camps were usually able to keep in touch with home to some degree. 'Before me,' wrote the Revd William Odom in 1917, 'is a large pile of letters from camp, trench, and hospital, telling of hardship, privation, and suffering, but all radiant with hopeful courage. Written in

---

THE COLLECTION THIS WEEK IS FOR

THE SHEFFIELD PRISONERS OF WAR
HELP COMMITTEE.

This Appeal CAN only be made to Sheffield people as the Funds are used only for the relief of Sheffield men. The first duty which the Committee concern themselves with is to see that the prisoners are as far as possible supplied with BREAD, and when this is assured other wants are dealt with.

Some of our men have been in prison since August 1914. Some have died there. It is absolutely necessary that nutritious foods over and above the War Supply should be sent to KEEP THESE MEN ALIVE.

The Treasurer (Colonel Chadburn) states that £130 was spent last month on this work. One halfpenny per passenger this week would relieve the Committee of anxiety regarding Funds for a considerable period.

PLEASE ALL HELP TO SEE THIS DONE
by placing your Contributions in the Boxes on the Platforms.

REMEMBER! ONE WEEK ONLY.

TRAMWAYS DEPARTMENT, DIVISION ST.   14th MARCH, 1916.

Egypt, Salonika, the Dardanelles, "Somewhere in France", or elsewhere, by dear Church lads …' Letters of hope and of gratitude telling of narrow escapes or of painful loss were all a way of keeping in touch with the life the men had left behind. With press censorship from the start, local papers soon began running letters from soldiers overseas as a way of telling readers what was going on. At first they tended to use those that supported the propaganda line and told of unspeakable atrocities by the dreaded Hun but slowly, in an age before telephones and social media, they began to evolve into a way of passing on news of local men to family and friends.

Often, the best a man could do was to send an official 'Field Postcard' with set phrases already printed on it, crossing out the ones that did not apply. It was short and impersonal – any other additions would mean it would be destroyed. At other times, he could write a letter that would be censored by his officers to ensure no information might be leaked to the enemy. From time to time, he could also get the coveted Army Form W8708 – a green envelope that would not be opened by regimental officers in which he could write about more personal and private matters. These links with home were treasured reminders that there was a life to go back to, but the harsh realities of trench life means few letters from home survived the rain, mud and need for toilet paper. These letters home, though, always received with the fear they may be the last, were kept safe. If a man was killed, a formal letter would be sent by his commanding officer with the basic details, often followed by other letters from friends who were with him at the end. It is letters like these that give us some idea of what life at the front was like.

In November 1914, Private Frank Barnes, a Sheffield man serving with the 2nd Battalion of the Warwickshire Regiment, wrote home. His unit had been involved in hard fighting and he described the shock of finding British soldiers who had been murdered after surrendering during the retreat from Mons. His unit counter-attacked to take their objective at bayonet point. He was amongst those detailed to round up any remaining enemy:

SHOT AT DAWN
Seven Sheffield soldiers are known to have been executed by the British Army during the First World War. In all, 3,080 death sentences were passed by British courts martial, of which all but 346 were commuted. Of these, 91 men were already under suspended sentence for previous offences, 40 of these having already been sentenced to death for earlier desertions.

Presently I got another shock. I was standing near a party of fifteen Germans when all at once one turned round and said in excellent English: 'Excuse me, but is there anyone here who comes from Sheffield?' Well, you can fancy how I felt, as I was the only man from Sheffield as all the other chaps came from Brum. After I had recovered my breath I got into conversation with him. He was not so old, and told me as much about Sheffield as I knew myself. 'Damned fighting,' he said, 'let me get back to England and my wife and children. I have been trying to get captured for several days and have only just succeeded.'

Hundreds of Germans had worked in Britain before the war, many as waiters, and spoke excellent English, frequently holding shouted conversations with the Tommies opposite to ask about news from their old home towns.

Elsewhere, in 1915, Edmund Yerbury Priestman, former leader of the 16th (Westbourne) Troop at its base at 473 Glossop Road, kept in regular contact with home. At the start of the war he placed his group at the disposal of the Sheffield Watch Committee and was appointed to supervise the widely scattered Scout guard camps until October when he accepted a commission in the 6th Battalion, York and Lancaster Regiment. Throughout his training he sent letters to his mother and to members of his old Scout troop describing the daily realities of life in the army. On 6 August 1915 he took part in the 'Yorkshire Landing' at Suvla Bay in Gallipoli and wrote home soon afterwards:

You must try and imagine us … squatting on our haunches in a shallow and dusty trench, listening to the most appalling uproar you could dream of. Behind us our big guns are roaring, above us the shells are tearing through the air, and in front of us, all up the long valley ahead, the crash of their bursting is simply deafening. Somewhere (all too vaguely described to us) are three lines of Turkish trenches which must be taken to-day.

But the valley is broad and thick with bushes, and the enemy is cunning to conceal his position. No matter! This terrific bombardment will surely overawe him and make our advance a simple matter. So we sit and listen and wait for the hour to come when we are due to hurl line after line of British Tommies against those trenches.

Can you picture the feelings of all of us as we watch the minute-hand slowly creep towards three? Ten minutes only now. Now only seven.

And what of us all when that hand shall have touched the half-hour?

The dentist's grisly waiting-den, the ante-room to the operating theatre – these multiplied a thousand-fold in their dread anticipation.

Edmund Priestman,
1890–1916.

And now the moment has come. A whistle sounds – a scramble over the trusty parapet we have learned to know as a shield for so many hours, and the valley is before us. 'Whiss! whissss!' The air is full on every side with invisible death, 'Whisss! phutt!' A bullet kicks up a little spray of dust from the dry grey earth underfoot, another and another to left and right. The sensation of terror is swallowed in an overwhelming conviction that the only possible course is forward – forward at any cost. That is what we have been telling ourselves all through the long waiting, and that is our only clear impression now. Forward – and we instinctively bend as one does to meet a hailstorm, and rush for it.

The landings failed to achieve the hoped for breakout and Edmund settled into the routine of trench life. A few weeks later, he tried to describe what it was like spending day after day under Turkish fire.

Afternoon Tea

Gallipoli Peninsula

Of course, being the celebrated Yorkshire landing, Suvla is much better run than anywhere else! And even here things aren't too good. This is not the Suvla it was in August; what with mules and stores and the other modern conveniences they have planted here there might not be a war on at all. The trenches themselves are getting monotonous, too, and you have to walk about half a mile from here to get any real excitement. We do sometimes get shelled where my dug-out is, but on top of the hill they get it every day. I went paying calls the other day, and the man I went to call on said : 'You'd better come inside, the shells are due about now.' Well, he'd hardly spoken before a big shrapnel came along – whizz! … We both dived inside his dug-out and he lay on top of me (me being the visitor – there's etiquette in these things), and so escaped being hit. The next that came along blew about four sandbags on to us, and my pal remarked: 'They'll really start in a minute!' Well, I was simply quivering with emotion as it was. Anyway, we put the sandbags back, and the next shell dropped slap into a group of fellows about ten yards away, blowing all the money out of one man's pocket and part of him along with it – horrid splash. The other man, an officer of one of the regiments in our brigade, simply vanished in a cloud of dust and we only found unimportant parts of him when we came to have a look round. Regular jigsaw puzzle he was, so we finally gave it up. By this time I was quite abject in my terror, and when they told me that a Taube [enemy aircraft] was coming over I simply set off and ran like a rabbit down that hill. It turned out to be one of our own machines, and they caught me and brought me back to have a cup of tea with them. Owing to the shelling, they said, their tea-parties were losing popularity and they weren't going to miss a visitor when he did come. But I didn't make what you would call a really good [guest].

In December, his old troop held a fundraiser sale to raise money to keep the group going and Edmund sent sketches of life at Gallipoli and some poems to be auctioned. Then the following appeared in the 5 February 1916 edition of the *Sheffield Daily Telegraph* …

A thrilling account has come to hand of a gallant stand made recently at Suvla Bay by a party of the 6th (Service) Battalion York and Lancaster Regiment, under the command of Second-Lieutenant E. Y. Priestman. This will be of interest locally, as a very large percentage of the recruits raised for this Battalion were residents of Sheffield and district. Lieutenant Priestman was a Sheffield Scoutmaster.

The account says: 'Our trenches ran along the coast, near Jeffson's Post, and orders had been received for us to work along the furthermost sap to enable us to gain a portion of higher ground on the left of our sap. In order to do this it was necessary to leave our trenches at night, run forward with sandbags to the place marked, and dig in as rapidly as possible. On this particular night, Lieutenant Priestman and about thirty N.C.O.'S and men were detailed to make good this position.

Leaving the trenches about 10 a.m. they gained the position without incident, and commenced to entrench as quietly as possible. Shortly afterwards the Turks rushed the position. Lieutenant Priestman did not retire, but opened a rapid fire, which kept the enemy at bay for a while, but, coming on again with a combined rush, they decimated the whole of the gallant little band. Lieutenant

Priestman fell, fighting till the last, and Regimental Sergeant Warr was also killed whilst taking up a message to him. We attacked the position again in larger force next night, and succeeded in holding it. The bodies of Lieutenant Priestman and several men were discovered, all the wounded having been removed by the enemy. The captured position was named 'Priestman's Post' by Headquarters, to commemorate the gallantry of this young officer, who was respected by all who knew him.

He is buried in Hill 10 Cemetery, at Suvla Bay. He was 25.

As Lieutenant Priestman arrived in Gallipoli, the men of the 12th (Service) Battalion, York and Lancaster Regiment (Sheffield Pals) were reaching the end of their training. In December they – along with their neighbours of the Barnsley Pals – set sail for Egypt as part of the Mediterranean Expeditionary Force, but as the Gallipoli campaign drew to a close, their orders were changed. In March 1916, they boarded ship in Port Said and sailed instead for France.

British trenches near 'Yorkshire Landing' at Gallipoli.

   In June 1915, the French commander-in-chief, General Joffre, had proposed that the Allies should begin to combine their efforts in a more effective way and it was agreed to form a permanent committee to co-ordinate action. Soon after that, Joffre proposed simultaneous large-scale attacks with maximum force by French, British, Italian and Russian troops as soon as conditions were favourable in the New Year. In January 1916, Joffre told the newly appointed General Douglas Haig that he wanted the British to attack north of the Somme on a large scale around mid-April 1916 to cause as much damage as possible to the enemy as part of a war of attrition intended to grind down the German forces rather than to break through their lines. Haig replied that he could not agree: his forces would not be ready, it would be politically unacceptable at home and the British public would regard it as a failed attack. After further discussion, Joffre agreed to change the plan, deciding that a combined Franco-British offensive should be carried out across

Members of the City Battalion shortly before sailing for Egypt, 1915.

the Somme sometime that summer, with a smaller attack by the British in the area between La Bassee and Ypres. Haig, aware of the recent developments in the design of the tank, hoped to wait until August so that he could use them to maximum effect in the British attack.

Unfortunately, on 21 February 1916 the Germans struck a mighty blow against the French at Verdun and it was soon clear that this was not a limited effort. The German commander, Falkenhayn, had set out to 'bleed France white' by attacking the symbolically crucial forts at Verdun to draw the French Army into a battle, the sole purpose of which was to kill as many Frenchmen as possible. On 3 March, Joffre asked Haig to do all he could to divert German reserves away from the battle, if necessary

Colonel C.V. Mainwaring, first commander of the City Battalion at the Civic Farewell, 1915.

by launching the Somme Offensive early. By the end of the month, Haig's senior, General William 'Wullie' Robertson – a man who had joined up as a private and now held the most senior position in the army – pressed the British Government for instructions about what they wanted Haig to do. On 7 April, approval was given for British involvement in the Somme Offensive.

On 29 May, at the suggestion of Haig, Sir William Robertson reminded the government that in view of the small number of French and British divisions available for the offensive, far-reaching results should not be expected. The idea of a simultaneous Allied attack with maximum force was no longer a possibility and the most that could be achieved would be to inflict enough damage on the Germans that they would have to pull back from their attacks at Verdun. Two days later, having been informed that Verdun was about to fall, Haig informed his French colleagues that the British would be ready to play their part. On 3 June, he received orders from Joffre that he must attack on 1 July.

The Sheffield Pals, now part of 31st Division, were tasked to attack the fortified village of Serre on the left flank of the British assault. In the weeks leading up to the attack they went through detailed training behind the lines until by the end of June they felt sure they were ready. Douglas Cattell recalled:

> I had always been a churchgoer. In fact I sang in the Sheffield Cathedral choir, boy and man, so I thought I would go for communion before the battle. Up to that point the forthcoming event hadn't bothered me, but at that church service held in the wood, seeing as we could the build up of marching men, guns and horses moving towards the front, then I had this feeling of awe. It must have been the effects of the service and seeing all this movement that you got this feeling, just as if something was coming at you.

That evening, men from Sheffield, Barnsley, Leeds and Bradford sat quietly around the village of Bus-en-Artois as the regimental bands serenaded them with tunes from home. Soon, it would be time to move forward.

On the morning of 1 July 1916, whistles blew along the British front line and the men of the Pals battalions went 'over the top' for the first time. The battalion's war diary sums up what happened next:

> 7.30am – Barrage lifted from the German front line and first and second waves moved forward into the assault. They were immediately met with very heavy machine gun and rifle fire and artillery barrage. The left half of 'C' Company was wiped out before getting near the German wire and on the right the few men who reached the wire were unable to get through … A great many casualties were caused by the enemy's machine guns; in fact the third and fourth waves suffered so heavily that by the time they reached No Man's Land they had lost at least half their strength. Whole sections were wiped out.

Moving up a communication trench on the way to the front.

At 8.21 p.m., the battalion reported to HQ 'Strength of battalion – ten men unwounded ...'

Nearby, 21-year-old Lieutenant Philip Howe of Sheffield had graduated from Sheffield University in the summer of 1914 and was invited in August to join the University Officer Training Corps. After just one month, he and several others decided instead to enlist as privates in the new Sheffield City Battalion. When it became obvious that the battalion would not be going into action soon, Howe applied again for a commission. His law degree stood him in good stead; the desperate need for officers in the Kitchener Army battalions meant he was granted an immediate commission and, without any training, he found himself a second lieutenant in the 10th West Yorkshires. Ever eager, he would lead the attack on Fricourt:

The trenches we had to get out of were deep, and it was necessary to climb up ladders. Naturally this made us a bit slow, so the people who came up behind suffered many more casualties than those who got over first. I put down my survival to the fact that I was first over the top, and got almost as far as the German trenches before anything happened. I met a German officer whose idea was to attack us as we crossed no man's land and he was armed with a whole array of stick bombs which he proceeded to throw at me and I replied by trying to shoot my revolver. I missed every time and he missed with his stick bombs as well. After this had gone on for a few seconds – it seemed like hours – somebody kindly shot this German officer and I made my way to the place I was told to go originally, which was a map reference about a hundred yards behind the German front line.

'Over the lid'. Troops begin the advance.

An assault wave goes into action. Troops following on behind were heavily laden with spare ammunition and weapons to reinforce the first wave.

I made my way to this little trench which I had seen by aerial photographs. I had started off with more or less the whole battalion, but I found myself in this trench with about twenty men. I had been shot through the hand and we quickly discovered that we were surrounded on all four sides. So I got all the men down in a dugout which had very steep sides and twenty steps leading down from the trench at the top to the dugout below. Just then another officer came along who had been shot through the leg and wasn't particularly mobile.

I sat halfway up the dugout steps. I was not able to shoot because I was shot through the hand, but the other officer, who was only shot through the leg, was able to shoot, so he lay at the top of the steps looking down the trench both ways, shooting the Germans as they came around the corners. The men down below loaded the rifle, handed it up to me and I handed it up to him.

It seemed a very long time before anything happened but just as our ammunition was running out, some English troops came down the trench from our left and they said, 'Oh, what are you doing here?' We tried to explain but they said that there were no Germans within miles. I told them that the Germans were just around the corner but they wouldn't believe me, and they turned the corner and I heard the crash of bombs. Me and my men ran the other way. What happened to the other people, I don't know. We went back to our own lines. The rest of the battalion who had followed me over the top at the beginning were all casualties. The few men I had got left were all that was left of the entire battalion.

GOING OVER THE TOP

I will now … explain to you the part played by a mere Tommy in an attack. We start about two days beforehand and draw extra iron rations (consisting of bully beef, tea and sugar and very hard biscuits) and also a pick or shovel and two bombs [grenades].

Then there are various inspections of ammunition, rifles, field ambulance dressings and steel helmets etc. As the 'day' approaches, the platoon officer parades all his men and speaks to them something like this; 'Now men, in a day or two's time I shall have the somewhat doubtful pleasure of leading you over the lid. I shall do my best to act as an officer should, and if anything happens to me I want you to take command in order of seniority. Each section commander knows what to do and I want you fellows to back him up and help him to do it…' There are murmurs from the irrepressible ones of 'hear, hear' and then a list of the next of kin of each man is taken just in case. Then the order comes round, 'packs in the [Quartermaster's] stores at 5pm, fall in at 7pm … at 7pm you fall in, in 'fighting order' … you then proceed to march up to the trenches and when you get to the first of these the order is silence, and no smoking. By 3am you arrive like a lot of shadows at the assembly trenches from where you are to start the stunt and catch old Fritz unawares… a certain time is fixed and called 'Zero'. That minute is the one in which the first wave mounts the parapet … we will call ours 4.10am. At about 4am a desultory shelling by our artillery is converted into an intense bombardment and is carried on until 4.10am. At 4.05am the platoon, already divided into a complete fighting unit (about 40 strong) of bombers, rifle grenade men and rifle men begin to get excited as the moment draws near. The last few minutes is [sic] the windiest … of the whole affair, the suspense makes it feel like an hour. A hissing whisper comes from the officer, although if he shouted he would not be heard owing to the rattle and crash of shells and machine guns, but like everybody else he is feeling the suspense, and no doubt thinking of his girl somewhere in Blighty. He says 5 minutes to go, 4, 3, 2, 1 now boys….

OVER

With that simple little word all feelings are banished and you scramble out of the trench and walk towards a yellow glare, like a great bonfire which is really the flash of the shells comprising our barrage. These barrages are a terrible curtain of fire poured into Fritz's front line by our guns of all calibres and our gallant Machine Gun Corps and their cheeky chatter … The idea (and it usually works all right) is to make him seek shelter of course, he is then at our mercy. That accounts for the large number of prisoners being taken. When a dugout is captured there are generally between 50 and 60 in one haul. Three or four of our men act as escorts for this lot to the rear of our lines … Although I have recently taken part in five attacks I cannot really analyse my feelings while actually crossing 'no man's land'. One sees all his pals dropping around him and unconsciously says to himself 'poor devils' and the next second is splitting his sides with laughing at a man who has been wounded and whose only object is to get to the shelter of our lines before the hubbub ceases and the snipers get to work. While all this is going on you never think of stopping but walk on unconcerned as if walking down High Street. No doubt if a thought of danger entered one's head he would get down into one of the numerous shell holes knocking about which offer excellent shelter. As soon as Fritz gets it into his thick square head that trouble is approaching in big numbers he starts to retaliate and then the noise is deafening … When the objective has been captured the first feeling is of thirst and a desire for a smoke and the next of pleasure at having taken part in a successful stunt. Then comes the nerve trying time when you have to dig a trench under fire and prepare to receive any counter attack … after that comes a tedious waiting for the party who are to relieve those who have been 'over the top'.

12/1357 Pte Harry Bertaut, Sheffield City Battalion

FIRST DAY OF THE SOMME
By the end of 1 July 1916, the Sheffield Pals had lost 248 officers and men killed, with 17 more dying of their wounds in the following week. In all, 468 men were reported as dead, wounded or missing in their first battle.

By the end of the day, the battalions proudly raised by local communities were gone. Back home, teenage girls were working for the Post Office delivering telegrams from the War Office. Margaret Furniss, 15, recalled:

… We used to go to the houses with mostly distress telegrams, you know, people whose lads had got killed or injured or something like that and it was a bit distressing then … the neighbours and that would stand in groups and as soon as they saw you of course your uniform was enough to set them off … they'd say 'oh a telegram girl' and then hang around to see what it was like and then more often than not the person you'd taken it to would be too nervous to open it and she would ask you to open it for her. If it was that someone had got wounded they'd burst out crying and you came away and left them with the neighbours.

Replacements prepare to leave for France.

After delivering sometimes devastating news, telegram girls were expected to ask, 'Will there be any reply?' Day after day they made their deliveries to Sheffield homes.

For those who survived came the grim task of passing on the news. 'It was a harrowing time for me,' Douglas Cattell remembered, 'with the mothers of my friends asking for information about their sons. When I told them they had been killed or were missing they wouldn't believe me. In fact in some cases it cost friendships.'

Replacements arrived to fill the ranks of the 12th Battalion but the unique character of the Pals was lost. The devastated survivors fought on. It would not be until the Germans pulled back in 1917 that the City Battalion finally reached their objective for the 1 July attack. 'Reg' Glenn was there:

Between September 1914 and 1918, 445 men were recorded as being killed serving with the 12th (Service) Battalion York and Lancaster Regiment (Sheffield Pals).

'Yorkshire Company', No. 5 Convalescent Camp, Cayeux. A special camp for new arrivals deemed not yet ready for battle, July 1918.

The Padre asked me if I would accompany him to visit our old front line and No Man's Land, which was littered with British dead. Ours were in lines where they had fallen. They were just skeletons in khaki rags and their equipment. We walked up to the old German wire. The Padre had brought a friend with him and the three of us turned back to look towards our lines. Then the Padre said a prayer for the dead and we sang Hymn number 437 from Hymns Ancient and Modern, 'For All the Saints'. I've still got that hymn book, it holds a very poignant memory for me. Next morning the dead were buried by an overnight fall of snow. It was to be some weeks before No Man's Land was cleared when V Corps began to make new cemeteries to lay our friends to rest.

By 1919, Sheffield men had written home from the Western Front, Gallipoli, Italy, Egypt, Greece, Bulgaria, Russia, Africa, India and the Far East. Sailors had fought at Jutland, off the Falklands and chased German raiders across the Pacific. It was truly a world war.

5

'OFT TIMES IT HAS BEEN DIFFICULT ...'

In the first week of war, the government passed a short but far-reaching piece of new legislation:

(1) His Majesty in Council has power during the continuance of the present war to issue regulations as to the powers and duties of the Admiralty and Army Council, and of the members of His Majesty's forces, and other persons acting in His behalf, for securing the public safety and the defence of the realm; and may, by such regulations, authorise the trial by courts martial and punishment of persons contravening any of the provisions of such regulations designed—

(a) To prevent persons communicating with the enemy or obtaining information for that purpose or any purpose calculated to jeopardise the success of the operations of any of His Majesty's forces or to assist the enemy; or

(b) To secure the safety of any means of communication, or of railways, docks or harbours; in like manner as if such persons were subject to military law and had on active service committed an offence under section 5 of the Army Act.

(2) This Act may be cited as the Defence of the Realm Act, 1914.

A photographer's pass is checked. Under DORA, civilians could find themselves arrested by the army for a bewildering array of offences.

The Defence of the Realm Act, or DORA as it came to be known, would expand over the coming years and affect the daily lives of every man, woman and child in the country. It would become illegal to fly a kite or whistle for a taxi in the street for fear they might be signals for enemy aircraft; wasting food or feeding bread to animals would be a criminal offence, as would melting down gold or silver. Owning binoculars could land you in court, as could speaking in a foreign language on the telephone. In 1916, lighting a match in the street during a Zeppelin alert cost one man a month's hard labour in prison. Undercover police officers toured local pubs to catch anyone foolish enough to try to order a round of drinks – a crime

CIVILIAN CASUALTIES FROM ENEMY ACTION IN THE UK 1914–1918			
Airship raids	Men	Women	Children	Total
Killed	217	171	110	498
Wounded	387	431	218	1036
Aircraft raids				
Killed	282	195	142	619
Wounded	741	585	324	1,650
Naval raids				
Killed	55	45	43	143
Wounded	180	194	230	604

for which the penalty could be £100 fine or six months in prison. Others investigated claims of food hoarding against anyone able to obtain what neighbours considered more than their fair share, again risking a fine or custody. Special Munitions Courts were set up to try cases of absenteeism from work and other offences deemed to be affecting the war effort. In May 1917, one typical example was Henry Johnson, a crane driver from Arundel Road in Handsworth. Johnson was fined £1 each for 'using abusive language' at work, 'interfering with other workmen' and 'losing time'. The court heard how he had arrived ninety minutes late for work and 'used filthy language when spoken to, and threatened to lay his foreman out and lame him'. Week after week, reports from the munitions court sat alongside those from the police courts, as anyone deemed to not be pulling their weight became a convicted criminal. Usually, these matters were dealt with at a local level but any offence under DORA could be tried by court martial and, in theory at least, if it was deemed that they were committed with the intention of helping the enemy, the penalty could be death.

AIR-RAID CASUALTIES

Elizabeth Bellamy (57)
Richard Brewington (11)
Ann Coogan (76)
William Guest (32)
Beatrice Hames (22)
Horace Hames (14 months)
Levi Hames (23)
George Harrison (59)
Vera Harrison (13)
Eliza Ann Harrison (48)
Albert Newton (28)
Alice Newton (27)
Elsie Mary Rhodes (4)
Nellie Rhodes (28)
Martha Shakespeare (36)
Sarah Ann Southerington (41)
William Southerington (37)
Frederick Stratford (49)
Margaret Taylor (39)
Albert Tyler (8)
Amelia Tyler (5)
Ernest Tyler (11)
John Tyler (2)
Joseph Henry Tyler (14)
Joseph Henry Tyler (45)
Selina Tyler (41)
Thomas Wilson (59)

Zeppelin Raids

On 23 September, German sources reported that a Zeppelin raid had hit Sheffield. The next day the local papers happily dismissed this obvious and crude propaganda as nonsense. 'The German account,' noted the *Telegraph*, 'is full of the usual mis-statements'. Then, on the night of the 25th, a German airship, the L-22, crossed the British coast. In Sheffield, warnings went out but this was the fourteenth alert so far without any bombs falling. Some residents fled the city, while some took official advice and went down to their cellars. Others, like Thomas Wilson of 73 Petre Street, were sceptical of the Zeppelin threat; Thomas told a neighbour that Zeppelins would never come to the city. He was wrong.

At about 12.20 a.m., L-22 flew over Fulwood and Redmires and then turned east towards Attercliffe, accelerating to full speed and zigzagging to avoid anti-aircraft fire. There wasn't any: the crews had no orders and their officers were away at a dance. The first bombs, two incendiaries, were dropped around 12.25 a.m. and fell in Burngreave Cemetery, near to the Melrose Road entrance. Other than scorching some grass and a notice board, there was no damage. Then a high-explosive bomb fell in Danville Street, killing Frederick Stratford, who was struck by shrapnel whilst in bed. In nearby Grimesthorpe Road a bomb fell on No. 112 and exploded, killing Ann Coogan and her daughter, Margaret Taylor. Back at Petre Street, the sceptical Thomas Wilson had gone to bed but heard the exploding bombs and rushed to his bedroom window. As he looked out, a bomb fell on a nearby outbuilding. He was struck on the chin by a bomb fragment and died instantly. The next bomb fell on Writtle Street, where splinters hit Elizabeth Bellamy in the back as she rushed across her bedroom. She was taken to the Royal Hospital, where she died three hours later.

Two bombs fell on a block of three terraced houses at Cossey Road. In No. 28, Alice and Albert Newton were killed as they lay in bed. Luckily, their infant son was spending the night with his grandmother in a nearby street and was unharmed. George and Eliza Harrison lived at No. 26 with their two daughters

Schoolchildren are taught what to do in an air raid.

and two grandchildren. After the warning had sounded, they were joined by William and Sarah Southerington, their neighbours from No. 24. George and William stayed in the living room while everyone else took shelter in the cellar. All eight were killed in the explosion. In a cruel twist, the Southeringtons' house suffered only minor damage and had they stayed at home, they would probably have survived. The second Cossey Road bomb landed on No. 10 killing Levi and Beatrice Hames and their 1-year-old son, Horace.

In Corby Street, a high-explosive bomb demolished No. 142, killing Selina and Joseph Tyler and their five children. The same bomb also killed 11-year-old Richard Brewington of No. 134 Corby Street and fatally injured Martha Shakespeare of No. 143, who died later in the Royal Infirmary. At Woodbourne Hill William Guest, a Corporation wagon driver, was killed in the street by a bomb as he tried to warn the occupants of a house that they were showing a light. The bomb fell within yards of where he stood. Huge numbers of people fled the city that night and for several nights after, fearing the bombers would come back.

THE RAID OF 25 SEPTEMBER

Details of the attack could not be published until December 1918, when the list of damage was released:

Street	Houses damaged	Deaths
Attercliffe Rd	3	
Bacon Lane	12	
Britannia Rd	2 (by fire)	
Corby St	4	9
Cossey Rd	6	13
Danville St	9 + 1 hotel	1
Earldom St	4	
Forncette St	2 (by fire)	
Grimethorpe Rd	7	2
Kilton St		1
Petre St & Earldom St	4	1
Princess St	Chapel and cottages	
Writtle St	3	1
Trent St	12	
Washford Rd	10	
Woodburn Hill	8	1

One day in late October 1914, 51-year-old Arthur Walby left his home in Woodseats to travel to Doncaster on business as a salesman for a Glasgow biscuit company. Sitting on a tram next to a soldier he struck up a conversation, talking – amongst other things – about his son, who had just joined the Sheffield City Battalion, and his nephew in the Royal Artillery in Aldershot. A few minutes later, Arthur was arrested and marched through the town to a military guardhouse by two soldiers with bayonets fixed to their rifles and followed by a crowd shouting 'German!' and 'Spy!'. There he 'was supplied with refreshments' but told he matched the description of a suspected spy seen the previous day wearing a green hat like the one Walby was now wearing. For the next twenty-two hours he was kept under guard, describing his captors to the press a few days later: 'They had bodies but that they had minds and spirits was not so evident … The language of some was characterised by a limited vocabulary but set off by a remarkable repetition of two words.'

Asked to summarise what he had learned from his experience, Arthur said, 'the wheels of justice grind slowly and when in Doncaster don't wear a green hat or ask military questions'.

One of the most evident effects of DORA was on the nation's drinking habits. In the nineteenth century, Sheffield earned itself a reputation as a hard-drinking city. Doctors noted that file grinders who drank heavily lived longer than those who didn't, simply because they were often too drunk to work and so breathed in less of the toxic dust that caused so many of their colleagues to die of lung disease by the age of 40. Absenteeism from work due to drink was endemic in heavy industry and it was not uncommon for men to drink before shifts, since pubs were generally open from about 5.00 a.m. until past midnight. When war broke out, the problem escalated. As industry stepped up production, overtime working became common but far from increasing production, in some cases it actually slowed. Investigation showed that men were able to earn enough over a weekend to keep them in beer for the rest of the week and so many simply didn't turn up for two or three days. The Admiralty complained that shipyard work that had taken one or two weeks in peacetime was now taking double that and more. The Chancellor of the Exchequer, David Lloyd George, claimed that 'drink is doing us more damage in the war than all the German submarines put together' and later added, 'we are fighting Germany, Austria and Drink and, as far as I can see, the greatest of these deadly foes is Drink'.

Determined to address the problem, one of the earliest measures under DORA was the order that:

> The competent naval or military authority may, by order, require all premises licensed for the sale of intoxicating liquor within or in the neighbourhood of any defended harbour to be closed except during such hours as may be specified by the order.

It was quickly followed by an extension of the restrictions to the area around any military establishment. As a munitions centre, Sheffield found itself covered by the new licensing laws. Opening hours were reduced to just twice a day, from noon to 2.30 p.m. and 6.30 p.m. to 9.30 p.m., and these restricted hours would remain in force for decades to come. Even this, though, was not enough. British industry was failing to keep up with War Office demands and, in 1915, further measures were introduced to try to curb drunkenness. It was already an offence under DORA to buy drinks for members of the armed forces 'with the intent of eliciting information for the purpose of communicating it to the enemy, or for any purpose calculated to assist the enemy; or ... when not on duty with the intent to make him drunk or less capable of the efficient discharge of his duties'. From October 1915, it became an offence to buy anyone a drink under the notorious 'No Treating' rule. Buying a drink for a friend or even family member could now lead to a fine of up to £100 or six months' imprisonment. Reactions to it were mixed. Some viewed buying rounds as a working-class practice and argued that the custom of having to pay for drinks for friends and acquaintances caused men to spend more on drink than they might normally. The 'No Treating' rule would, they said, 'free hundreds of thousands of men from an expensive and senseless social tyranny'. Not everyone saw it that way and the message from government was mixed – whilst efforts were being made to control drinking, the Ministry of Munitions itself openly regarded brewery staff as 'war workers' in its own propaganda material. A secret war began between drinkers who had no intention of giving up enjoying a sociable pint with their workmates at the end of a shift and the police tasked with enforcing the law. Undercover police officers visited pubs on the lookout for anyone breaking the rules and prosecutions began across the country. Most pubs at the time had waiter service and, if treating was allowed, the drinkers, the waiter and the landlord could all face hefty fines or imprisonment, so great care was taken to ensure that if a man bought two pints at the bar, the landlord would stand by him to watch him drink both. If someone at a table bought three bottles of beer, he would be given just one glass.

One hidden side effect of the rules affected the least rowdy customers: many horses, mules and donkeys used for delivery work around the town had become used to being given the odd drink themselves. Now, buying a pint for a donkey was technically illegal. As one disgruntled delivery man explained:

If they're goin' to rob t'donkey of 'is beer, it'll mean secret drinkin' in the stable. I shall have to take t'beer 'ome. But it's goin' to be an 'ard job tearin' t'donkeys away from,

> the pubs ... They've never given any trouble on licensed premises, and I've never seen one any the worse for a drop too much – not that you could mek one drunk if you tried.

Determined drinkers found a loophole: buying a drink over a meal for a dinner companion was allowed. Soon every pub offered meals, although, as one report explained:

> It looks as though the military authorities will sooner or later have to define what a 'meal' is. At the present time there is a tendency for the sandwich, which masquerades as a meal to get thinner and thinner; nothing could well be finer or more gossamer-like than the shaving of ham within the thin slices of bread. The price of this 'meal' varies from 3*d* to 4*d*.

The pub sandwich, often recycled to serve several customers, became the subject of jokes about the man who ate the sandwich and ruined the pub's trade or about the meal being carried off by a fly. In October 1916, despite the best efforts of undercover police to enforce alcohol laws, the House of Commons heard that Sheffield was still 'scheduled as a drunken area'.

Pubs, of course, did some of their best business at weekends, particularly after a football or cricket match, but they too were under threat. Thousands of men flocked to join the colours but many thousands more did not. Some were opposed to the war, while others fell short of the medical standards required or were too young or too old. Men with jobs or businesses had to consider their long-term prospects and others needed to decide whether their families could survive the loss of income a soldier's wage would bring. Soon tensions emerged between those who went and those who stayed behind and arguments raged about who should go. Most controversial of all was the question of what sportsmen should do. Was it was right that fit young men were playing or watching games while their contemporaries were fighting for the country's survival? Some believed that all professional sports should be cancelled immediately, and others that they were 'a national necessity', vital for maintaining morale at home and in keeping with the government's insistence that people should carry on as normal. Cricket and racing, both in mid-season in August 1914, were the first to come under criticism, but both argued that they were contractually obliged to continue for the time being. By 1914, professional sports were big business and the Football Association fought hard on behalf of its members to argue that matches were ideal recruitment venues and so served a useful purpose – itself supporting the view of opponents that footballers ought to set an example, not leave it to others to go in their place. Rules were hastily consulted and changed to allow players who did join to play for their units and even their clubs if they were based nearby but also to allow players to re-sign for their clubs after discharge from the army or navy, both previously forbidden. Against widespread opposition from the sections of the press and others, the season got under

As the 1914/15 season got under way, Sheffield United began their journey to the FA Cup against Chelsea.

OUR HEARTS .BLEED FOR THE OLD MAN.

Sheffield United : " My word ! they have been knocking you about ; where was it, Mons or Marne ? "
The Pensioner : " Neither, 'twas at Park Royal, Middlesbrough, and somewhere else not a hundred miles from here."

THE MUD SLINGERS

The Leader: "Come on, boys, keep it up, some of it's bound to stick."

["The Times" declare that Professional Footballers are shirking their National Duties and that League Matches are a scandal and prevent Recruiting.]

way on 1 September 1914 when Sheffield United lost 3–2 to Sunderland. It was not a great start but by the following April they were favourites to win the FA Cup Final, to be played on 24 April against Chelsea at Manchester's Old Trafford ground to avoid congestion around London. The *Sheffield Telegraph* complained that United were 'bringing shame on themselves and the city' by taking part but 49,557 people turned out to watch (with the *Manchester Guardian* pointing out that those watching who were not in uniform perhaps should have been) as United beat Chelsea 3–2. The 'Khaki Cup Final' drew a line under the arguments. From July, players were placed on amateur status, paid expenses only and professional football was suspended for the duration of the war.

A few days after the Cup was shown to the crowd at the Wharncliffe Cup Final, and as if to emphasise events elsewhere, on 1 May 1915, the Cunard liner RMS *Lusitania* set sail from New York bound for Liverpool with almost 2,000 passengers

Professional sportsmen, and especially footballers, found themselves the target of criticism for continuing to play games when men were fighting and dying in France. The pro and anti camps were bitterly divided.

PLAYER'S CIGARETTES

COOK · ENGLISH · GOUGH · STURGESS · UTLEY · BRELSFORD · SIMMONS · EVANS · FAZACKERLEY · KITCHEN · MASTERMAN

ASSOCIATION CUP WINNERS
SHEFFIELD UNITED. 1915

Sheffield United's cup-winning team. After the 'Khaki Cup Final' of 1915, professional football was suspended. Sheffield would hold the cup until 1920.

and crew aboard. The German Embassy had published warnings in the New York papers for American citizens not to sail with her as she was now designated an 'auxiliary cruiser' by the German Navy, who claimed she was carrying war supplies in contravention of the so-called 'Cruiser Rules' and therefore a legitimate target for their submarine patrols. At about 2.10 p.m. on 7 May, 11 miles off the coast of Ireland, the *Lusitania* sailed into the path of U-boat *U-20*, which launched a single torpedo, striking the ship on the starboard side. Moments later, a second explosion inside the *Lusitania* blasted out her hull and just eighteen minutes later the ship's bow hit the seabed whilst her stern was still above water. Of the 1,959 passengers and crew, 1,195 died. The attack provoked outrage worldwide and widespread attacks on German shops and businesses across Britain. On 10 May, the *Sheffield Telegraph* wrote of all Germans as a 'breed of bestial savages animated only by a terrible lust for blood'. A few days later, a mob gathered on Attercliffe Road …

First to be attacked was Fred Carley's shop at No. 85 Worksop Road, where 'a host of women invaded the shop and pulled down all the hanging hams and made away with them … some of the women went upstairs and continued the work of destruction there'. Fred's mother, 51-year-old Sophia, had been born in Germany but had lived in Britain for over twenty years.

As the riot grew, 'rather furious altercations' took place between the mob – described as being mainly 'women, girls and young boys' – and the two police constables on patrol in the area at the time. Traffic was stopped as the crowd grew and marched on Herbert Leech's shop at No. 583 Attercliffe Road

Across the country, violent mobs attacked any suspected German families.

where, by the time they arrived, a Union Jack was flying. It meant nothing. The windows were shattered and as their neighbours ransacked the home, 'several female members of the crowd had possessed themselves of bunches of black puddings and polonies, politely requested a Press photographer to take a snapshot of them, which he obligingly did'.

An intrepid reporter for the *Star* managed to get to the Leech family as the mob moved on. They had barricaded themselves in one room and escaped without injury. As Herbert spoke to the reporter, a shop assistant brought him news of the damage. '"Oh my God", exclaimed Mr Leech, "surely they have not taken my mother's clock". He then burst into tears and said "this is what they do to an Englishman's home – my mother's clock is gone … it would take two of them to carry it." He could say nothing more being overcome with emotion.'

His two daughters managed to escape the crowd and made it back home safely. Herbert Leech was born in Bethnal Green and brought up in Chesterfield but his wife, Barbara, had been born in Germany. Under the terms of the 1870 Naturalisation Act, she was legally British.

So it went on: Bullinger's shop on Attercliffe Common was next, then Hanneman's at No. 855 Attercliffe Road where superstitious rioters smashed everything but the mirrors that lined the shop's walls. Worksop Road, Newhall Road and Woodbourne Road all suffered attacks. Winifred Burnet from Bromley Street heard about the riot and went to check on a friend whose home had been targeted. Seeing the damage, she took her friend home with her by taxi but as soon as they got back, Winifred's home also came under attack and her friend fled 'where, we don't know'. She wrote to the *Telegraph*:

I am an English girl, and am continually taunted with the expression 'you blooming German spy', 'you rotten German spy', 'German refugee' and similar expressions … people have promised faithfully to lynch me and someone else is going to break my jaw … what I did was a mistaken kindness I know … In these days we must think before we act. I have lost my eldest brother in the war. By that we've suffered enough without any more. I am certainly English, for which I thank God, though one cannot help their nationality.

The people of Sheffield reacted angrily to the rioters. Commenting on the women involved, 'Vulcan' wrote to the *Telegraph* that, 'I am thinking they would be much better employed in cleaning their houses. I do not know how they could find time on Friday mornings ... I hope the authorities will make them replace everything they have stolen. There are things in everyone's home one values, German or not.'

On 28 May, fifty-three 'men, women and lads' appeared before magistrates Mr J.C. Clegg and Colonel H. Hughes, charged with theft. The ringleaders who had led the attack had not been identified and when one defendant laughed about it and claimed he was simply carried away by patriotism, a furious Colonel Hughes rounded on him: 'Did you think it was patriotic to turn yourself into a thief because a German had got money?' Frustrated at having only the relatively low-level offenders, and angry that those targeted had been British families with legitimate businesses, Hughes said, 'the whole thing is a disgrace to Sheffield'. Each defendant was fined 20*s* (about £70).

Herbert Leech's clock was recovered safely a few days after the riot. Attempts to have all those regarded as German regardless of age, gender or actual legal status interned were ignored by Sheffield Council and a request to the Tramways Committee to post anti-German posters was refused.

More anger surfaced after the city was bombed in an air raid in September 1916, with damage to eighty-six houses, a hotel and a chapel. Twenty-four men, women and children aged from 14-month-old Horace Hames to 76-year-old Ann Coogan, were killed outright. Four more victims died later of their wounds and another fifteen people were injured. By the standards of what would come to the area a quarter of a century later, it was a light raid. To people who never dreamt that the war would come to their doorstep, it was a terrifying experience. Panic alerts were sounded twice in a single night in the week after the raid. Wartime censorship prevented the reporting of the raid until December 1918.

Even after the attack, though, not everyone could find it in themselves to hate. On Wednesday, 20 March 1918, Corporal Smith of the Royal Flying Corps was on duty guarding prisoners of war about to set out to work at a quarry just outside Sheffield. He noticed one of the prisoners scribble something on a piece of paper, put it in a matchbox and hide it behind some water pipes. A few minutes later, a Women's Auxiliary Army Corps (WAAC) girl working at the POW camp picked up the matchbox, pocketed it and went to her workplace in the camp.

Even the most hard-hearted sometimes struggled to see all Germans as Huns. Several Sheffielders, knowing their own men were held in Germany, found themselves in court for sharing food with hungry prisoners.

Corporal Smith reported the incident and kept watch over the next few days. The same thing happened on 22 and 23 March, at which point Smith arrested the girl, who turned out to be Florence Mayos, aged 23, from Weston Street in Sheffield, and took her to the adjutant. On Monday, 25 March the Sheffield magistrates remanded Mayos on bail and her trial began on Wednesday, 3 April 1918 .

The story began three weeks earlier when Florence, or Florrie as she was usually known, had been walking along with her friend Winifred Dean, also a WAAC. Winifred told the magistrates that a matchbox had landed on the ground in front of them, thrown over a wall in the prison camp by a grinning German soldier. In it was a note addressed to 'My Darling Unknown'. Laughing about it, the girls had told their friends about the secret admirer and Florrie had decided to send a message back. It soon became a running joke and one box contained the gift of an aluminium

Coal rations being delivered.

ring inscribed with the prisoner's initials, 'H.R.' in German script. One witness, identified as 'Mrs Sergeant King', gave evidence on Florrie's behalf that she had been serving with the WAAC since leaving her job on the Corporation Trams because of ill health. Winifred testified that Florrie had been open about the letters and that all the girls working at the camp thought it was a joke. Florrie herself told magistrates that it was simply to 'cheer him up'.

When Detective Inspector Fretwell visited the camp he had found that the prisoner must have been very cheerful. Two letters in Mayos' handwriting were found on him, another signed 'L', a fourth came from a Sheffield girl called 'Lily' and a fifth and sixth were signed 'Flossie'. Satisfied that there was no intent to help the prisoner escape, the court fined Florrie £5. What her fiancé, a soldier based in Ripon, thought about it is not recorded.

For those left behind at home, life changed irrevocably, especially under DORA, sometimes for the better, often for the worse. Some of the changes it brought are still with us today: daylight saving time was introduced in May 1916, the same year that saw cocaine possession made illegal (previously it had been available over the counter and had even been packaged as 'The Soldier's Friend', sold to help troops stay alert in the trenches). Licensing laws that would remain in force for generations were brought in and rationing introduced to try to fairly allocate sparse food supplies so that poorer families actually ate better in wartime than they had in peace. Wages doubled and measures to control rents prevented landlords from evicting the families of serving men. The Home Front of the Second World War is well known but largely forgotten now is that all the elements so familiar from books and films about the 1940s began with just two short paragraphs in August 1914.

Since its foundation in 1660, the British Army had been a small volunteer force that fought wars in far-flung outposts of empire. People were aware of it, but most members of the British public had no real connection with it. Now, for the first time, war had reached into the homes of the majority and had come to the streets of Britain. In 1917 the Revd Odom of Heeley recorded what it was like to be part of a community so deeply affected:

> It has been of deep interest to find how many of the fallen I baptised and married. Said a mother who had lost her son: 'You married me, you baptised my four children, buried two, and married the one now killed.' Another to whom I had given a memorial card said: 'This is the third kindness you have done – you married me; you baptised my boy, and now you have given me this.' Again and again in visiting the bereaved, sorrowing, and anxious, I have been deeply touched, and oft times it has been difficult to find words of comfort and consolation.'

As the war entered its fourth year, for those at home there was little to do but wait and hope.

6

Sir Jonas and the Blue Death

The last year of the war began with a compulsory 'meatless day' and for the rest of the war, on at least one day per week, no meat could be sold anywhere in the city. By 3 January, 20,000 men were on strike over pay and workers of the Sheffield Gas Company were threatening to join them, leading one angry local to write, 'I never thought the day could have dawned on which I am almost as much ashamed of being English as I should be of being a German. The Germans do keep their treacheries for their enemies; the striker bestows them on his own kith and kin and his own nation.' By 7 January the strikers had won a 12.5 per cent pay rise and returned to work just as tea and margarine were made subject to rationing. As the food supply dwindled, canteens were opened to provide cheap meals for workers in factories and a Food Control Committee was set up to oversee rationing, but although there were clearly shortages, the local newspapers argued that the move was not necessary. Sheffield, they said, was no worse than surrounding towns and in many cases better off. In Rotherham, for example, the papers reported:

> Scarce though food is, there is nothing to justify the spectacle of the needs for hundreds of people waiting for up to four hours at a time for the staple foods of tea, sugar or butter. Children and mothers with babies in arms were in these queues. Many women having got supplies would then join the back of the queue to be served again. Others who were late arrivals would find the food had been sold out when it was their turn.

As H. Middleton, a Boy Scout in 1917, later recalled, 'If we were walking up the road and saw a queue at a shop we used to stand in it … to see what they'd got and whatever it was we used to get some'. Prosecutions for selling certain goods at over the regulation price began with Ellen Waller, a grocer from Attercliffe, for charging over a shilling above the maximum 4s per pound for tea. Neighbour began to spy on neighbour and court cases involving food hoarding were regularly reported. Each week, the committee announced the ration for the coming week in the local press: by October it was down to '8oz sugar, 1oz butter, 4oz margarine, 2oz jam, 2oz tea, 2oz lard, four meat coupons value 4d each'. Sheffield was the only place in the country where jam was rationed, but the good news that week was that beef sausages would be available, although the meat content had largely been replaced by breadcrumbs, cereal and water, making the sausages explode when being cooked. By the end of the war they had been given a new name – bangers.

In February, the Sheffield City Battalion was formally disbanded as part of a reorganisation of the army and the men posted to other units. A few weeks later, the Germans launched a major offensive that almost broke through the British lines and thousands of men were reported missing, though most were later found to have been taken prisoner. In response, with the British Army ordered to stand and fight to the last man, munitions workers agreed to forgo their Easter holiday to make up shortages caused by earlier strikes – even the unions condemned those who refused. Local volunteers were among those drafted to the East Coast in case the attack was the prelude to a full invasion, by then a seemingly unlikely but not impossible event. So great was the crisis that the government was forced to lower the minimum age limit for service overseas from 19 to 18 years 6 months in order to replace its losses, rushing thousands of teenage conscripts to France.

But the tide was turning. In April 1917, the United States had entered the war, although at the time its tiny army could do little to help. Over the past year, it had expanded to a formidable force and in May 1918, Sheffield turned out to welcome the

American troops arrived in June 1918. Exhibition baseball matches drew huge crowds to Brammall Lane and extra games were played at Hillsborough.

first contingent of 450 American soldiers to arrive in the city. To celebrate Independence Day, a sports-starved crowd of 16,000 turned out to watch a baseball match between contingents of the US Army and Navy – an event that proved so popular that the navy team stayed on and another was held two days later at the Wednesday ground, where Sheffield dignitaries were introduced to the 'truly American custom' of chewing gum, 'the joy of which is said to become intensified by constant practice'. Wrigley's gum had been on sale in Sheffield for years but had not yet caught on with the high and mighty. In 1910, the *Telegraph* had reported that a third of Americans were addicted to 'this strange practice' and one man, hauled before magistrates in London, claimed that he had been given gum by some American sailors and it was this that had made him appear drunk when arrested.

In August, Septimus Bennett attended the first 'Grand Sports Day' arranged by the Vickers Ltd Holme Lane Works Social Club on grounds on Wood Lane. 'Little else has been talked of at the works for a week or so,' and the handicapping of competitors for various events had caused headaches for the committee given the physical condition of many of the workforce. Having studied the list of events, Septimus decided he would have no chance in the tug of war against the team of blacksmiths put forward and was too young for the 'Veteran's Race' for men aged 45–74. The sack race, he felt, would be embarrassing and the egg and spoon (which he believed he could manage) was only open to girls. The event took place on a sunny afternoon with the work band playing and 'very much resembled a country fete', despite being only a couple of miles from chimneys belching out smoke. Watching the girls in 'very short navy blue skirts' compete in the skipping race, he considered it 'a wonderfully attractive exhibition of legs and arms'. Against the blue sky and green fields, though, one colour stood out:

> Perhaps I have never seen so much black in the country on a bright sunshiny day. Quite a number of girl competitors had transferred a Black Brassard to their running costumes ... It was an afternoon of contrasts. At one time there might never have been such a thing as a war on, at another, we were forcibly reminded of it.

Sitting nearby was 'Curly', a young man of 20 years whose trip to France had lasted only six months but cost him a leg. 'His girl never left his side ...'

As the war began to look like the end might be in sight, businesses started to look to the future. In 1917, Alice Wheeldon, an anti-war activist from Derby, had been arrested on charges of conspiracy to assassinate the prime minister on the basis of evidence provided in secret by a discharged mental patient turned MI5 agent. The case prompted outrage and many believed it was little more than an attempt to justify the existence of the intelligence agency, which was under threat of closure at the time. In 1918, a similarly controversial case made headlines with the arrest of former Sheffield mayor Sir Joseph Jonas on charges of spying.

Born in 1845 in Bingen am Rhein, about 40 miles west of Frankfurt in Germany, Jonas moved to Sheffield in 1870 and by 1875 had set up business with a toolmaking company, Jonas, Meyer and Colver. He became a British citizen and by 1890 ran one of the city's most successful firms and stood unopposed as town councillor for Attercliffe. In 1904 he was knighted and became Lord Mayor of Sheffield. He was, it seemed, the epitome of the immigrant made good.

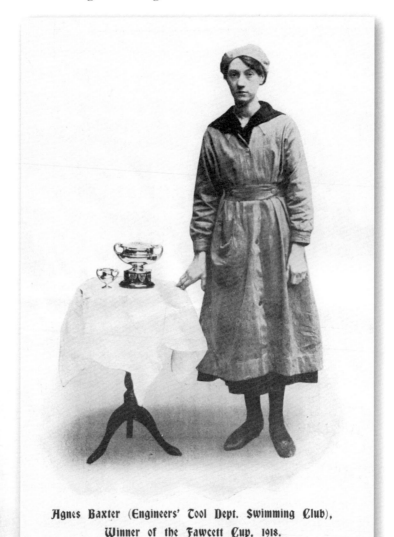

Munitions factories created their own sports teams. By 1918, these included women's football teams.

Agnes Baxter (Engineers' Tool Dept. Swimming Club), Winner of the Fawcett Cup, 1918.

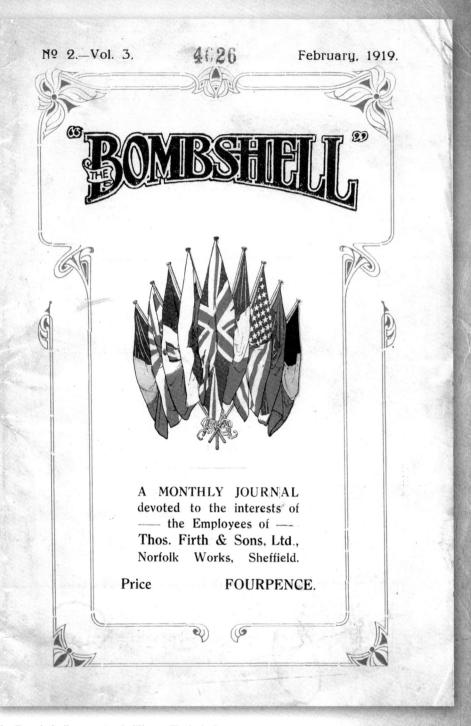

Nº 2.—Vol. 3.   4026   February, 1919.

"BOMBSHELL"

A MONTHLY JOURNAL
devoted to the interests of
—— the Employees of ——
Thos. Firth & Sons, Ltd.,
Norfolk   Works,   Sheffield.

Price   FOURPENCE.

The Bombshell, *magazine for Thomas Firth & Sons.*

In late 1913, Jonas was contacted by Paul von Gontard, a member of the Prussian House of Lords and director of the Deutschen Waffen- und Munitionsfabriken – the German equivalent of the British Ministry of Munitions. Gontard was interested in a planned new rifle to be designed and made by Vickers in Sheffield and wanted to find out more about the project. Jonas had known Gontard for over thirty years and such requests in the business world were not unusual. British and German arms manufacturers were in fierce competition for overseas markets but also frequently shared information and equipment. Krupp, one of Germany's main weapons producers, used forges and machines made in Sheffield and Vickers used German-designed fuses in its explosives. Although the British media were increasingly paranoid about German spies, the request was not seen as suspicious and Jonas contacted one of his directors, Charles Alfred Hahn of Wolstenholme Road, to ask for any information about the planned site and size of the factory and about any orders that might be in the pipeline. It was not detailed and amounted to the sort of information any company might seek about its opposition. Hahn (who changed his name to Vernon at the outbreak of war) in turn asked Richard Zieschang, a German-born employee at Vickers, to gather the information.

When war broke out, Sir Joseph felt that his civic work spoke for itself and so he did not need to prove his loyalty, but actively encouraged German-born Sheffielders to find ways of showing theirs. When, in 1916, a local steel magnate, Edgar Allen, bequeathed £5,000 (about £300,000 in 2014) to the University Applied Science Department, Jonas matched the donation to fund the Allen and Jonas Laboratory for material testing. Then suddenly, at the age of 73, Jonas was arrested and charged with conspiring to 'obtain and communicate certain information prejudicial to the interests of the State and information useful to the enemy, and information relating to prohibited places and things therein'. The trial became a national sensation and was even reported by the *New York Times*.

As the *News of the World* reported:

MrTindal Atkinson, King's Counsel for Sir Joseph, said his client took upon himself the sole responsibility for obtaining the information, which was in no sense intended to assist a possible enemy. Sir Joseph's sole purpose was to satisfy the inquiry made by a large customer, who, unfortunately, was in Germany, as to certain matters connected with a firm that was about to open business in competition with Gontard. It was deplorable in the interests of justice that this case should be tried in reference to matters which took place nearly five years ago, and nearly a year before the outbreak of war. Mr Justice Lawrence said it would be most unjust for the jury to allow their minds to be prejudiced against defendants because of the monstrous conduct of the Germans in this war, of which neither they nor anyone else in 1913 dreamed.

After seventy-five minutes of deliberation, the jury found Jonas and Charles Vernon not guilty of 'conspiracy to injure the interests of the State' but guilty of obtaining information relating to a prohibited place. Jonas was fined £2,000 and Vernon £1,000, but Sir Joseph's disgrace was not over yet. Within a week, it was announced in the House of Commons that his case would be submitted to a committee on the British Nationality and Status of Aliens Bill. In other words – if the Bill became law – to consider whether he would be stripped of his citizenship and deported from Britain. A few weeks later, it was announced that the king had 'degraded' Jonas by taking away his knighthood. Then Sheffield removed his name from their list of Justices of the Peace.

Many, though, saw his fall from grace as the result of political dealings. Jonas had lived in Sheffield for forty-eight years and was a successful businessman who had done what all businessmen did. As a leading steel manufacturer, he had links around the world and had been asked by an old and valued customer for the sort of information all businesses gathered about their competitors long before war between Britain and Germany seemed possible. His prosecution, five years after the event, came a year after the Royal Family had finally renounced its own German heritage and after the University of Sheffield had removed Julian Freund's Chair as Professor of German whilst he was interned as an enemy alien without having committed any crime other than to teach languages at the university since 1908.

The stress took its toll. After a lengthy legal battle with the Home Office, Joseph Jonas died from a stroke in 1921. It is perhaps a measure of the feelings of many in his adopted hometown that large crowds of mourners attended his funeral. Among those present were the Lord Mayor and Master Cutler, representatives of the university, the Sheffield Education Committee and the Chamber of Commerce. To the very end, his workforce still referred to him only as 'Sir Joseph'.

Meanwhile, in France, 8 August had gone down as a 'black day for the German Army' when Allied forces inflicted a crushing blow. Everywhere the Germans began to pull back and the final offensive began. Fighting took place not in trenches but across open ground and in the shattered villages of northern France. In some of the costliest fighting of the war, British troops were making advances unheard of in the past few years. Throughout August and September, the losses were heavy but at least there were clear signs that the deaths were achieving something.

Thoughts turned to what would happen when the war was over. Plans were put in place for a memorial hall to take pride of place in Barker's Pool but even as the building was being discussed, news broke that two pigsties near Tinsley Park Road were being used as homes. A man, his wife and their two children shared one, while another couple lived nearby. Appalling as that might be, what made it worse was that both men were discharged soldiers, one of whom had been wounded three times while serving in France and who had been unable to find anywhere else to live. As one letter writer put it, Sheffield contained housing that was 'not fit for pigs or Huns' and demanded that better town planning be made to build homes for returning heroes. The chairman of the Corporation was later quoted as saying that in fact it was not as bad as it had been reported. The family were, in fact, living in a shed for which they were paying rent of 1s a week. Whatever the truth, it did not bode well for the return of many more men from the front.

In March, a short epidemic of flu had swept Britain. In October it returned with a vengeance. Neutral Spain had no press censorship and reported it fully, thus giving it the nickname 'Spanish Flu'. It soon gained a far more sinister name from the effects of the disease on breathing. As victims struggled to get air, cyanosis set in, draining the colour from the lips and face. People began to refer to 'the blue death'. With so many men called up, public services struggled to cope with the epidemic and Sheffield Corporation had to intervene to gain exemption for its gravediggers as bodies piled up. It was claimed that the dead were sometimes left lying in their homes for over a week until a burial could be arranged and on 6 November it was reported that 468 people had died in the previous week alone – more than the Sheffield City Battalion had lost in the entire war.

News of the end of hostilities came as the epidemic was at its height. Another 402 victims died in the week that the Armistice was agreed and news of Sheffield men dying in field hospitals added to the list. Still, air-raid 'buzzers' sounded, bells rang and, despite the fears of infection, crowds gathered in the city centre to celebrate a day many thought might never come. The munitions works closed and, for the first time in years, streetlights blazed and fireworks were set off. The cathedral remained open until 11 p.m. to allow Thanksgiving services to be held. In France, the reaction was often more muted. For some young men whose whole adult life had been given over to the war, there was a sense of anti-climax and the worry about what would come next. For most, though, the main concern was to return to civilian life as quickly as possible. It was not going to be easy.

Sheffield's Refugees Return Home

With the war over, France and Belgium also started to rebuild. Families forced out early in the war came back to find their homes and businesses gone, sometimes struggling even to identify where their homes had been. Some never returned, the empty plots standing like missing teeth in villages even now. There had been talk of leaving the old front line as a memorial, but the farmland was too valuable. Making it safe to work would claim more lives and even a century on, the 'iron harvest' of shells plucked from the fields claim more victims every year.

In January 1919, it was time for Sheffield's refugees to go home. They had become part of the community and, despite the jokes about 'Belgian atrocities', most were sorry to see them go. 'Ally', an employee at Thomas Firth's, was one. Given short notice, he was preparing to leave when his co-workers presented him with an engraved watch. He told them:

> I am exceptionally sorry that I have to leave all this behind … but I shall of course be glad to get back amongst my own parents and countrymen in Belgium. I shall never forget the kindness which you showed me in trying to forget as much as possible the terrible agonies of mind through which one must necessarily pass in such a case as mine. Again, ladies and gentlemen, I must thank you … I can assure you that this kindness to me will also be felt by my people, when I am able to tell them of the object of this gift and the pleasant times I have had during my four years amongst you in Sheffield.

The next day a train full of refugees left Sheffield for the journey home, Mrs Van Roosbroeck, of Antwerp, spoke to the *Telegraph* and *Star* about the people of Sheffield. 'They are a splendid lot,' she said, 'and I have had a very happy time amongst them. I shall always remember my happy time in Sheffield. In fact, I won't be allowed to forget it, because my boy speaks English perfectly. Good luck to the girls of Sheffield.' 'At least twenty Belgians took with them Sheffield girls as wives,' reported the *Daily Independent*, 'whilst conversely a number of Belgian girls remain behind having married Sheffield men.'

A memorial to Belgian refugees, City Road Cemetery. (Beth Lynch)

THE BLUE DEATH
The Spanish Flu epidemic of 1918–20 killed an estimated 20 million people worldwide and earned its grim nickname from the effect it had on oxygen supplies in the body. Sheffield suffered particularly badly in a wave that struck as the war was coming to an end:

Week ending	Deaths reported
30 Oct	233
6 Nov	468
13 Nov	402
20 Nov	241
27 Nov	164

The war was not yet over. True, the firing had stopped, but Germany had not yet surrendered. There was still the possibility that they might resume hostilities. That meant keeping an army ready. Despite the continuing threat, by January 1919 men were being discharged at a rate of 10,000 per day, but this was not fast enough for many and soldier strikes became regular events at base camps in France. Some were spontaneous demonstrations, others part of a co-ordinated campaign by trade unions like the Calais Area Soldiers' and Sailors' Association to organise protests about working conditions, poor food and slow demobilisation. At Folkestone, thousands of troops returning from leave refused to board ships for France, whilst the following news reached Australia (in the *Northern Territory Times and Gazette* of 11 January 1919):

[f]ive thousand members of the Army Service Corps broke camp at Brentford and commandeered four lorries. Part of 300 of them reached London and created a demonstration of a good-natured character before the War Office. They protested against the delay at demobilisation. It is understood that the Government has decided that the army service corps shall be demobilised in concurrency with other units. Ten thousand soldiers were being demobilised daily during the past week. It is expected that the figure will soon become 20,000.

Addressing complaints about demobilisation, Secretary of State for War Lord Milner explained:

Remember that, though the fighting may have ceased, all is not yet over. Impatience and overhaste might yet rob us of all that four long years of unexampled struggle and sacrifice have won. We have yet to make a just, strong and enduring peace. When the representatives of Great Britain go to the Council table to negotiate that peace, they must not have a disarmed and disunited nation behind them. If we are all at sixes and sevens at home, if what remains of our Army is not compact, disciplined, orderly, we shall never get the sort of peace, which we justly expect. The world, which is still in many parts seething with disorder, may not settle down for years, or let us get back to normal life and work in safety and tranquillity … Our guiding principle was to demobilise in the way most likely to lead to the steady resumption of industry, and to minimise the danger of unemployment. Pivotal men first, basic industries like coal mining before those of less vital importance. In each industry those men first, who were assured of immediate employment. Subject to these ruling principles, we want to release the older men, and those of longest service, before the younger ones. That is the general idea. I don't say that it can ever be perfectly executed. Certainly the execution isn't perfect yet. When the huge engine began to move, some defects immediately appeared in the machinery. These are being remedied. Some officials may have been stupid or obstructive. I am afraid, where thousands of people have to co-operate, there will always be a good sprinkling of muddlers. But when all is said and done the big engine is moving. It is moving at a steadily increasing pace.

Men were allocated to demobilisation groups, each subdivided into discharge numbers. First to go would be civil servants, who would then administer the system, followed by those who would create jobs for others. Next came 'slip men' with chits to prove they had work to go to, followed by those with good prospects of finding jobs. Many men who had chosen to leave work to volunteer in the heady days of 1914 were therefore among the last to be released, leading to even further discontent. For the older men,

In all, 5,752 Sheffield-born soldiers died as a result of the war, although the Corporation Roll of Honour lists only 5,085. Sixty-eight men are known to have died serving with the Royal Navy.

it would mean a return to the lives they had left behind, but many thousands were 19 years old and had come of age during the war. To them it was the beginning of their adult lives and they would have to start from scratch.

The process of turning these men back into civilians was mainly a bureaucratic one. Before each soldier left his unit he was – once again – medically examined and given Army Form Z22, which allowed him to make a claim for any form of disability arising from his military service. At the same time he was given Army Form Z44 (Plain Clothes Form) and a Certificate of Employment, showing what he had done in the army. A Dispersal Certificate recorded personal and military information and also the state of his equipment on discharge. If he lost any of it after this point, the value would be deducted from his outstanding pay. Any local currency had to be exchanged at an army post office for a postal order in sterling.

Passing back through an Infantry Base Depot, he would be sent to a Dispersal Centre in England, where he received more forms and a railway warrant or ticket to his home station. An Out-of-Work Donation Policy was issued, which acted as an

King George V visits Sheffield in 1918.

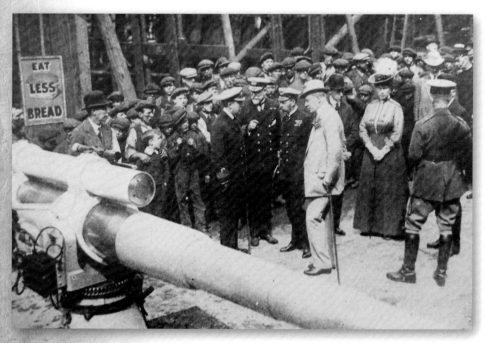

insurance against unemployment of up to twenty-six weeks in the year after he was discharged along with an advance of pay, a fortnight's ration book and also a voucher – Army Form Z50 – for the return of his greatcoat to a railway station during his leave. He could choose between being provided with a civilian suit on production of his Form Z44 or a clothing allowance of 52s and sixpence. In uniform and still holding his greatcoat and helmet, he then began his final leave. Still technically a soldier, he could now wear civilian clothes and could no longer legally wear his uniform twenty-eight days after leaving the Dispersal Centre. During the leave he had to go to a railway station to hand in his greatcoat and would be paid £1 for doing so as part of his war or service gratuity payment, with any other payments due to him sent in three instalments by money orders or postal drafts. As long as the Military Service Act was in force, all men liable for service who were not remaining with the colours in the Regular Army had not been permanently discharged or who were not on a Special Reserve or Territorial Force Reserve engagement were discharged into Class Z of the Army Reserve and were liable to recall to a designated base in the event of a national emergency.

Now all that remained was to come home and find a job.

Despite the impact of the First World War and the Spanish Flu epidemic, by 1921 Sheffield's population had increased to reach almost 512,000 people with an average of 7,700 births per year throughout the war.

'A Spectacle both Attractive and Inspiring'

The war with Germany formally ended with the signing of the Treaty of Versailles in the summer of 1919. On 17 July, special parties were held in parks across Sheffield with the council paying for tea, music, flags and medals for the children. Two days later, Saturday, 19 July was designated as 'Peace Day' and a day of national celebration. It began at noon with a march past of serving and discharged soldiers, sailors, airmen and contingents of women from the Royal Air Force, Royal Navy and Queen Mary's Army Auxiliary, each marcher receiving a card of thanks from the Lord Mayor. Throughout the day and into the evening there were bands and dancing in the city's parks and a special afternoon tea for widows and orphans. At 11 p.m., searchlights shone from the roof of the *Telegraph* offices and at Shire Green and around Sheffield the anti-aircraft guns fired a salute, the signal for bonfires to be lit at Bole Hills, Parkwood Springs, Ringinglow, Skye Edge and Wincobank and for rockets and flares to light the night sky. It would, the *Telegraph* promised, 'provide a spectacle both attractive and inspiring'.

But though the war in Europe might be over, Sheffield soldiers were still in action. British troops had been sent to Russia to support anti-Bolshevik forces and took control of Arkhangelsk in the Arctic and, alongside Japanese, American, Canadian, French and Italian troops, held the port of Vladivostok in Siberia. Among them was Sidney Cutts, a 24 year old from Woodhouse who died on 12 May 1919 from wounds he had received in action

Reindeer patrol, Russia, 1918–19.

a month earlier. He was buried in Onega in northern Russia and remembered on the family plot in Woodhouse Cemetery.

Harry Cherry, called up in late 1917 as an 18 year old, fought through the bloody Second Battle of the Marne as part of the King's Own Yorkshire Light Infantry and stayed with his battalion as it marched into Germany in the winter of 1918. He decided to stay on in the army and in 1920 was posted to Iraq. Although he didn't know it, also serving nearby were three of his former comrades, including Frederick Fox from Skinnerthorpe Road.

As the army struggled with the process of releasing its soldiers, employers at home began to lay off staff. The vast munitions industry needed to scale back and war industries closed down. It was agreed that men would be paid 24s a week unemployment pay with 6s for the first child and 3s for each of the others. Women were entitled to 20s, boys under 18 would receive 12s and girls 10s. It wasn't much compared to the wages they had been earning but at least it helped them along until something else came up. New homes were to be built and for a while the building trade picked up, but the British economy had suffered a shattering blow and jobs for returning veterans became increasingly scarce.

In all, 5,752 Sheffield men had died in the war. Many more returned disabled or physically ill. Arnold Loosemore, winner of the Victoria Cross and the Distinguished Conduct Medal, came home having lost a leg. He died in 1924 from tuberculosis. He was 27 years old. In the years to come, men succumbed to wounds contracted long before as infections developed in their wounds. Others returned sound in body, but scarred by their experiences.

The stress of trench warfare took its toll. When it was ordinary soldiers who broke down it was easy for doctors to dismiss them– as Churchill's personal physician had done – as 'miserable creatures from the towns' and to blame character defects. Eventually, though, even the best men found it too much and their breakdowns could not be ignored until it was agreed that there were two forms: 'emotional', linked to weakness in the individual, and 'commotional', caused by brain damage from the concussion of nearby shells – hence 'shell shock'. But the problems didn't end when the man left the battlefield. Often they could lay dormant for years until something – a firework, a car backfiring, a smell or some other trigger – brought it all back. It would not be until 1980 that American psychologists would find a name for what was happening to veterans years after their war was over: post-traumatic stress disorder, the problems of coming to terms with death and the horror of war. It was hard for men to talk to their families about what they had seen and done, so many banded together to form clubs where they could meet and talk to others who knew. At night for years afterwards, the streets of Sheffield sometimes echoed with the screams of men waking from nightmares. Two years after the Armistice, 65,000 former soldiers were receiving pensions for psychological problems and 9,000 still needed hospital care. Twenty years later, when Britain faced another world war, 120,000 veterans had been granted pensions due to the mental effects of the Great War.

As the euphoria of peace calmed down, Britain began to count the cost. The mammoth *Statistics of the military effort of the British Empire during the Great War, 1914–1920* published by the government in 1922, lay out in painstaking detail the expenditure

of ammunition (the bombardment before the start of the Third Battle of Ypres between 17 and 30 July used 4,283,550 artillery shells at a frighteningly precise cost of £22,211,380 14s 4d). Businesses, too, counted the cost. Massive profits had been made but now trade slumped on both sides. In July 1921, the German manufacturer Gustav Krupp filed a claim in Sheffield, asking £260,000 for the use of his Krupp-Patentzünder (patent fuse) by Vickers during the war. Krupp estimated that the British had fired 4,160,000 shells and killed a German with every other one.

Krupp's arms factory in Germany during the war using presses made in Sheffield.

Whether this was a boast about German efficiency or British accuracy is unclear but Vickers, of course, were reluctant to pay and claimed they had used just 640,000 shells. In 1924 Krupp referred the matter to the Anglo-German Mixed Arbitration Tribunal and in 1926 a compromise was reached that saw Vickers agree to pay a reduced amount. As the German economy collapsed, even though £40,000 was little more than a token payment, Krupp settled. Vickers had supplied Krupp with the machinery needed to produce weapons to kill British troops and Krupp supplied Vickers the technology used to kill Germans. It was just business.

In 1921, *Soldiers Died in the Great War*, a massive eighty-volume set of books produced by His Majesty's Stationery Office, listed 5,752 men born in Sheffield as having died in army service. More had been lost in the Royal and Merchant Navies and the Royal Air Force. Sheffield civilians had died in air raids and the bombardments of the East Coast, and an unknown number had been killed by the effects of war work. Memorials to the human cost began to spring up and it is a testament to Sheffield that the first permanent memorial was not to local men, but to those refugees and Belgian soldiers who had not survived their exile. In 1921 a monument was erected in City Road cemetery to commemorate their loss. In August 1923, Lieutenant Colonel Wedgwood unveiled a memorial stone at a ceremony outside Serre, attended by 150 of the surviving Sheffield Pals, and the village was 'adopted' by Sheffield. On 7 July 1923 the Sheffield War Memorial Committee proposed a competition to select the most suitable design for a war memorial to represent the City of Sheffield. E. Vincent Harris, the architect for the City Hall, was the judge and entries were restricted to architects and sculptors working, or with practices, in Sheffield. Thirty-four designs were

Private Arnold Loosemore (1896–1924) of Sheffield, awarded the Victoria Cross and Distinguished Conduct Medal.

PTE. A. LOOSEMORE,
West Riding Regt.

The unveiling of Sheffield's War Memorial, 1925.

submitted and the winners, sculptor George Alexander and architect Charles Carus-Wilson were announced on 7 March 1924. A fundraising campaign was launched with house-to-house collections, special fundraising performances at theatres, cinemas and other venues and flag days to find the £5,345 needed to erect the memorial in Barker's Pool.

Four bronze figures of soldiers, slightly less than life size, stand with their heads bowed and rifles reversed above panels showing the emblems of local regiments, Sheffield's coat of arms and the badges of the navy, merchant navy, army and air force. The original design included four female figures between the soldiers but in order to save money, they were removed. The soldiers' backs are to a central column that becomes a flagpole above their heads and the mast rises to the height of the nearby City Hall. It was made in one length of mild steel in Hull by Earle's Shipbuilders and Engineers and transported by rail to the Wicker in Sheffield, its final journey proving a challenge in the narrow congested streets of post-war Sheffield. It was unveiled on 28 October 1925 by Lieutenant General Sir Charles H. Harington, and came to be regarded as Sheffield's answer to London's Cenotaph as a site of public mourning for the thousands of young lives it represents.

The economies of Europe were shattered by the cost of the war. Men returned expecting a home fit for heroes, but found cash-starved councils unable to provide those homes. Exports plummeted because few countries could afford imported goods. Unemployed former soldiers scraped whatever living they could. Former colonels and majors found work as cooks and shop assistants.

When Douglas Haig, the commander-in-chief of the British Army – often remembered today as 'Butcher Haig' – died in 1928, veterans queued for hours in freezing conditions to file past his body as it lay in state. Hundreds of thousands lined the route of the funeral procession, as *The Times* put it, 'come to do honour to the chief who had sent thousands to the last sacrifice when duty called for it, but whom his war-worn soldiers loved as their truest advocate and friend.' When war broke out again, the ranks of the army and Home Guard were filled with veterans once more willing to defend their country.

It was only many years later, with the rise of the Campaign for Nuclear Disarmament in the early 1960s, that the image of incompetent military leaders really took hold. For the next forty years, the war would be remembered as a futile waste of life caused by generals who neither knew nor cared about the men in their command. It was not a war the veterans of the '20s and '30s remembered. They were not, they insisted, lions led by donkeys, because that implies that the men who went to war were too stupid to think for themselves. They had fought a war they thought to be right and they had fought it well. They had faced the horrors of the mud and the blood and they had won. They believed they had earned the right to be proud of what they had achieved.

In 1936, the site of the trenches from which the Pals set out on that fateful day twenty years earlier was dedicated as a memorial park. Today it remains one of the most visited of the many battlefields of the Western Front, but even so retains an air of peace and tranquillity. An immaculately kept cemetery marks the furthest point many of them reached that day and shards of metal from shells and bullets still litter the fields all around.

The remains of trenches dug by the Sheffield Pals on 'Hill 60' at Redmires on the outskirts of the city.
(Beth Lynch)

Bottom right in diagonal to top left and the darker grass in this image are trench lines. The dip in the image below is the remains of an unfilled but eroded trench. (Beth Lynch)

Schoolchildren come in groups to hear the stories of their ancestors and the noise they made on the coach becomes hushed. They walk to the cemetery and find names they know from home on graves of men old enough to be their brothers.

The Sheffield Pals reach out across a century to touch the hearts of a new generation and their story lives on.

SELECT BIBLIOGRAPHY

Books

Dalton, S., *Sheffield Armourer to the British Empire* (Wharncliffe Books, 2004)

Derry, J., *The History of Sheffield* (Pitman & Sons, c.1914)

Gibson, R. and Oldfield, P., *Sheffield City Battalion* (Pen & Sword, 2006)

Lomax, S., *The Home Front: Sheffield in the Great War* (Pen & Sword, 2014)

Philips, M. and Potter, J., *Septimus Bennett: Artist in Arms* (Pentland Press, 2001)

Scott, P.D., *Vickers – A History* (Weidenfeld & Nicholson, 1962)

Sparling, R.A., *History of the 12th (Service) Battalion, York & Lancaster Regiment* (J.W. Northend Ltd., 1920)

Newspapers

Sheffield Daily Telegraph
Sheffield Evening Telegraph
Sheffield Independent
Yorkshire Post

About the Author

Tim Lynch served in the Falklands and Northern Ireland. He now works as a freelance writer, specialising in history and travel. He is an active member of the Western Front Association and has taken part in archaeological work on the battlefields of France. He is a regular contributor to magazines such as *Britain at War*, *Military Illustrated*, *Skirmish* and *Stand To!*, and is the author of *Battlefield Archaeology*, *Silent Skies*, *Dunkirk 1940: Whereabouts Unknown* and *They Did Not Grow Old: Teenage Conscripts on the Western Front, 1918*. He lives in South Yorkshire.

Great War Britain:
The First World War at Home

Luci Gosling

After the declaration of war in 1914, the conflict dominated civilian life for the next four years. Magazines quickly adapted without losing their gossipy essence: fashion jostled for position with items on patriotic fundraising, and court presentations were replaced by notes on nursing. The result is a fascinating, amusing and uniquely feminine perspective of life on the home front.

978 0 7524 9188 2

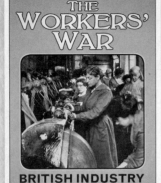

The Workers' War:
British Industry and the First World War

Anthony Burton

The First World War didn't just rock the nation in terms of bloodshed: it was a war of technological and industrial advances. Working Britain experienced change as well: with the men at war, it fell to the women of the country to keep the factories going. Anthony Burton explores that change.

978 0 7524 9886 7